RICHARD B. MANCKE

563

THE FAILURE OF U.S. ENERGY POLICY

COLUMBIA UNIVERSITY PRESS
NEW YORK & LONDON 1974

LIBRARY OF CONGRESS CATALOGING IN PUBLICATION DATA

MANCKE, RICHARD B   1943–
THE FAILURE OF U.S. ENERGY POLICY.

BIBLIOGRAPHY: P.
1. ENERGY POLICY—UNITED STATES.
2. ENVIRONMENTAL POLICY—UNITED STATES.
3. PETROLEUM—TAXATION—UNITED STATES.
I. TITLE.
HD9502.U52M35   333.7'0973   74–5253
ISBN 0–231–03787–2
ISBN 0–231–03853–4 (PBK.)

COLUMBIA UNIVERSITY PRESS
PRINTED IN THE UNITED STATES OF AMERICA
10 9 8 7 6 5 4 3 2

PREFACE

The United States is in the midst of a well-publicized but very real energy crisis. The crux of this crisis lies in the contradiction between economic, political, and technological realities and our policymakers' inappropriate responses. Energy policy has historically been hit and miss, partially because of the complexity of comprehensive policy formulation and partially because those who make decisions are not usually allowed to view the situation in a comprehensive framework. Whatever the reasons, we are now shackled with a frequently contradictory set of policies designed for a world our policymakers have misperceived.

Part I introduces this theme of contradiction and misperception by assessing the dimensions of energy problems presently facing the United States. It demonstrates that government action is necessary if the U.S. is to achieve three valuable goals: preventing a growing dependence on energy from insecure sources; reducing the environmental pollution that is a by-product of the production, distribution, and consumption of energy; and reducing the annual arbitrary transfer of billions of dollars from American taxpayers and oil consumers to owners of oil lands and residents of the major oil-producing states. Part II elaborates on this theme by presenting a series of case studies of the most important policies presently aimed at assuaging one or more of our energy problems. In fact, on balance, most have actually exacerbated them. This failure of policies costing several billions annually provides ample justification for the alarmed cries that the U.S. faces an energy crisis. Part III concludes on a positive note by outlining a comprehensive program of reforms and new measures designed to remedy past and present energy policy failures.

ACKNOWLEDGMENTS

In the course of conceiving and completing this policy analysis, I have become indebted to a great many individuals. Those deserving special thanks for offering information, comments, and criticisms that helped to directly shape the final product are Morris A. Adelman, C. David Anderson, Joseph Bell, Christopher Combest, Bernard Gronert, Barbara Hobbie-Mancke, Joseph Lerner, John Nivala, William Pierce, William Geoffrey Shepherd, and Thomas Stoel.

The contributions of M. A. Adelman and Barbara Hobbie-Mancke were especially influential. Professor Adelman's influence is not solely attributable to the scholarly works that establish him as the preeminent authority on U.S. energy policy. His much more personal contribution stems from those intangible personal qualities which prompted me to regard him as my intellectual mentor at M.I.T. Barbara Hobbie-Mancke's influence is only partially attributable to the close personal relationship between us. Equally important have been her contributions as co-author of much of the material in chapter 5 and as the hard-nosed critic and editor who demanded justification for every statement contained herein.

Jane Dodge, Gail Klein and Nicole Wing also deserve special thanks for their secretarial assistance.

RICHARD B. MANCKE

CONTENTS

I

DIMENSIONS OF THE U.S. ENERGY CRISIS

1. ADEQUATE PROVISION OF LOW-COST ENERGY   3
2. THE SECURITY OF U.S. OIL AND GAS SUPPLIES   17
3. POLLUTION   35
4. DISTRIBUTIONAL CONSEQUENCES OF U.S. OIL AND GAS POLICIES   46

II

CURRENT U.S. OIL AND GAS POLICIES

5. STATE AND FEDERAL LAND USE POLICIES   59
6. TAX INCENTIVES   77
7. OIL IMPORT POLICY   88
8. NATURAL GAS POLICIES   106
9. OTHER POLICIES   122

III

A NEW ENERGY POLICY

10. REFORMING EXISTING ENERGY POLICIES   141
11. NEW POLICIES   154
NOTES   163
BIBLIOGRAPHY   183
INDEX   187

I

DIMENSIONS OF THE U.S. ENERGY CRISIS

1.

ADEQUATE PROVISION OF LOW-COST ENERGY

TECHNOLOGICAL CONSTRAINT

In order to fuel its economy the United States requires enormous amounts of energy—72 trillion Btu in 1972. Crude oil and natural gas provide three-fourths of this total. Historically, U.S. energy demands have grown at a rate only slightly less than the rate of growth in real GNP. If this historical relationship continues, our energy demands will nearly double by 1985. The U.S. Interior Department predicts that, because of a lack of better substitutes, crude oil and natural gas will have to supply at least 65 percent of this much higher total (Table 1-1, p. 4). Should new nuclear power sources not be developed so quickly as the Interior Department optimistically predicts, the share of oil and gas would have to be even higher.

The historical constancy of the relationship between the rates of growth of energy demand and GNP has frequently been explained as being entailed by technology. The argument goes as follows: Energy is a key input required to produce many of the goods and services comprising GNP, therefore technologic constraints require that energy consumption grow roughly as fast as real GNP. The chief flaw in this argument is its failure to consider the likely effects of higher prices.

Over the past century the relative price of energy has fallen.[1]

Table 1-1 United States Demand for Energy Resources
by Major Sources, Year 1970 and Estimated
Probable Demand in 1975, 1985, and 2000 [a]

	1970	1975	1985	2000
Petroleum (includes natural gas liquids) [b]				
Million barrels	5,367	6,550	8,600	12,000
Percent of gross energy inputs	43.0	40.8	35.6	34.6
Natural gas (includes gaseous fuels)				
Billion cubic feet	21,847	27,800	38,200	49,000
Percent of gross energy inputs	32.8	32.4	29.5	26.4
Coal (bituminous, anthracite, lignite)				
Thousand short tons	326,650	615,000	850,000	1,000,000
Percent of gross energy inputs	20.1	18.2	16.7	13.4
Hydropower, utility [c]				
Billion kilowatt hours	246	282	363	632
Percent of gross energy inputs	3.8	3.2	2.6	2.6
Nuclear power [d]				
Billion kilowatt hours	19.3	462	1,982	5,441
Percent of gross energy inputs	0.3	5.4	15.6	22.7

SOURCE: Statement of the Honorable Rogers C. B. Morton, Secretary of the Interior,
before the Committee on Interior and Insular Affairs, United States Senate, June 15, 1971.

[a] Preliminary estimates by Bureau of Mines staff.

[b] Product demand; includes net processing gain.

[c] Includes pumped storage, internal combustion, and gas turbine generation. Converted
at prevailing and projected central electric stations average heat rates as follows: 10,769
Btu/kwhr in 1970; 10,000 Btu in 1975; 9,500 in 1985; and 8,000 in 2000.

[d] Converted at average heat rates of 10,769 Btu/kwhr in 1970; 10,500 in 1975 and 1985;
and 8,000 in 2000.

That is, energy has become relatively cheaper than most of the
other inputs used to produce GNP. As a result, it is not surprising
that many have found it profitable to substitute increased energy
inputs for other, more expensive, productive factors. If, instead,
energy prices had risen, there would have been fewer of these substitutions, and the observed rate of growth of energy consumption
would therefore have been less. Evidence from intercountry com-
parisons suggests that these price-induced savings could be large.
To illustrate: (1) Coking coal is much cheaper in the United States
than in Japan. As a result of these cost differences, the American
steel industry consumes roughly 30 percent more coal per ton of
steel produced.[2] (2) Largely because of excise tax differences,
most refined oil products cost roughly twice as much in Western

Europe as in the U.S. At least partially as a result of these cost differences (and the European practice of placing much heavier purchase taxes on larger, new cars), Europeans make more intensive use of fuel-saving mass transit. Moreover, the typical European motorist drives a car that gets roughly twice as many miles per gallon as the car driven by his American counterpart.[3] These dramatic intercountry differences suggest that it is a mistake to view the level of real GNP as the sole determinant of the level of energy demand; relative price levels are also important.

Suppose the relative prices of all types of energy were to rise sharply and additional rises in these prices were anticipated. Initially, even a large price rise would cause only a slight reduction in energy demand because there are only a few short-run substitutes. To illustrate, if energy prices were to rise appreciably, many citizens would take steps to reduce their energy bills. Among the most obvious are reducing home and office temperatures, driving less, and turning off lights in unoccupied rooms. The total reduction in energy demand as a result of these initial steps would be slight—primarily because the costs of larger reductions would be regarded, in most cases, as too high. Homes and offices would be judged too uncomfortable if their temperatures fell much below 68 F; suburban families would find it inconvenient to spend several additional hours each day walking, riding bikes, or waiting for buses; and none of us would want to unplug our instant-on color TVs at the close of each viewing day.

As time passed the price-induced fall in energy demand would grow far larger because additional and better substitutes would become possible. For example, those buying new homes and offices would opt for more insulation; growing numbers of new car buyers would choose to trade size, power, and perhaps even styling for greater fuel economy; and there would be a rising dependence on mass transit. In sum, even if energy prices rise sharply, the present linkage between levels of energy demand and GNP must remain rather tight in the short run because of a lack of economic substitutes; however, it will loosen considerably as time passes because a greater variety of energy-saving substitutions will become feasible. Since the main uses of energy are either to power or heat relatively long-lifed capital assets and durable consumer goods, the time required to complete most of the transition from short run to long run could easily exceed 10 to 15 years. The practical importance of this long transition period is that, barring the adoption of stringent energy-saving policies, levels of energy consumption will continue to rise only slightly less quickly than levels of real GNP throughout the 1970s.

United States energy policymakers are charged with the important responsibility of securing supplies of energy sufficient to meet the demands of a growing economy, and at the lowest possible costs. Implicit in this charge is acceptance of the premise that more growth is good. Energy policymakers are not in a position to challenge this premise. Nevertheless, since many outside the government have challenged it, it is necessary to assess its merits.

DESIRABILITY OF ECONOMIC GROWTH

In recent years a strong assault has been mounted against the government's presumption that continued economic growth is desirable. Arguing that the acquired tastes of most citizens are determined by the dictates of a few, several critics assert that the apparent wish of most Americans to enjoy ever-rising living standards does not imply that ever-rising levels of per capita consumption are really desirable. Many of these same critics go even farther and argue that a second but related weakness plagues the claim that economic growth is conducive to more interesting lifestyles. These critics ask rhetorically: Is this claim true in nations that have achieved "reasonable" living standards? Do the millions who consume most of their leisure time watching television really enjoy interesting lifestyles?

Increasing numbers of Americans are finding antigrowth arguments like these persuasive. However, in rebuttal, it is important to emphasize their elitist and paternalistic nature. This was done admirably in a recently published reminiscence by Professor Abba Lerner:

One of the deepest scars of my early youth was etched when my teacher told me, "You do not want that," after I had told her that I did. I would not have been so upset if she had said that I could not have it, whatever it was, or that it was wicked of me to want it. What rankled was the denial of my personality—a kind of rape of my integrity. I confess that I still find a similar rising of my hackles when I hear people's preferences dismissed as not genuine, because influenced or even created by advertising, and somebody else telling them what they "really want." [4]

The critics of growth believe that, besides overstating growth's benefits, growth's advocates systematically understate its total costs by excluding from their calculus any consideration of its costly by-products. Senator Henry Jackson summarized this sentiment when he noted that "economic indices are no longer viewed as the sole measure of progress. We are entering an era in which qualitative values and aesthetic factors are considered as important as material wealth." [5]

Because of their inherently subjective nature, it is difficult to evaluate many of the arguments against growth. The President's Council of Economic Advisers recognized this when it commented on the deficiencies of GNP as a measure of economic growth:

> For anyone whose values differ greatly from those of the general synthesis, the measurement of economic growth will be different from that commonly made. For anyone to whom clean water is the only valuable product there has been no economic growth since the time of Hiawatha. The argument is ultimately a matter of taste. [6]

Nevertheless, the President's economic advisers assert that since most Americans enjoy the current uses of growth's product, more growth is good. We have seen why growth's critics have asserted the contrary proposition. Fortunately, at least a partial resolution of this controversy is possible.

Suppose, only for purposes of debate, that growth's critics are correct when they charge that advocates of growth have overstated its benefits and understated its costs. Does this mean that more growth is necessarily bad? Because the assumed facts only support the contention that our society has misued growth's products, the answer must be no. More precisely, the chief argument for a nation's decision to encourage economic growth is that it increases the opportunities available to its citizenry. It does this primarily by raising the efficiency of the nation's scarce productive factors.

When economic growth is justified in this neutral way, almost no one finds it objectionable. This is because most growth critics are asserting that the fruits of past growth have been squandered—not that they are inevitably bad. Thus, when they attack continued economic growth in the United States, aren't they really attacking our society's decision to purchase more consumer goods and war material rather than more social service programs? Would they really be against growth if its fruits were used to achieve goals they desire? Most Americans would probably agree that more growth is good *provided* that its products are used in ways they regard as socially "useful." Thus, while this discussion may attack particular uses of growth's products as being socially wasteful, it will not attack the premise that, other things being equal, more growth is good.

A LIMIT TO GROWTH?

The U.S. government has instructed its energy policymakers that their chief duty is to adopt policies that will guarantee supplies of energy sufficient to meet growing demands. Is this feasible? A coterie of modern Malthusians conclude that it is not. Their conclusion is premised upon the familiar Malthusian syllogism that (1) since there are only finite physical supplies of the energy resources necessary to support all physiologic and industrial activity and (2) since the demand for these resources will continue to grow exponentially, therefore, (3) energy demand must, some day, outstrip the available supply.

According to the systems analysts who wrote the recent best seller *The Limits to Growth,* the probable progeny of this incestuous coupling of continued growth with limited resource supplies will be a sudden and uncontrollable decline in both population and industrial capacity within the next 100 years.[7] This conclusion rests upon the factual assumptions that present rates of growth in resource demand will continue unabated and that supplies of the economically important resources are five times as large as presently known global reserves. However, the authors claim that, even given the most optimistic estimates about either the rate of future technological progress or the ultimate size of the resource base, the grace period would be extended by no more than 100 years.[8]

Given the continued coupling of exponentially growing resource demands with finite energy supplies, some type of cataclysm is of course inevitable. In order to postpone this eventuality, the modern Malthusians urge the immediate adoption of policies designed to slow present and future rates of economic growth to a snail's pace. The cost of such no-growth policies would be enormous—$40 to $50 billion in 1973, and even more later. Are the facts marshalled by the Malthusians persuasive enough to justify such Draconian measures? Because exponentially growing energy demands are not an inevitable consequence of economic growth and because economic energy supplies are many times larger than the Malthusians suspect, this question deserves a negative answer.

Historically, growing economies have had exponentially growing energy demands. The principal causes have been exponentially growing populations and (see above, Technological Constraint) the discovery of so many new energy reserves that the relative cost of energy has actually fallen. Neither growing populations nor falling energy prices are an inevitable consequence of economic growth. In fact, if the energy supply situation is as bleak as the Malthusians suspect, energy prices must soon begin to rise sharply and world population growth will slow. In turn, the rate of growth of energy demand will certainly fall and could be reversed if the shortage is severe enough. Even if this chain of events occurs, more economic growth would be desirable. In fact, since economic growth increases the opportunities available to a nation by raising the productive efficiency of its resources, it would become more desirable if the Malthusians' energy supply projections prove correct. Will they?

The magnitude of our planet's economic energy resource base is, in fact, several orders of magnitude larger than the modern Malthusians' most optimistic predictions. The cause of their crucial underestimates is a misunderstanding of the economic nature of natural resource supply. Two interrelated phenomena explain why economic supplies of all natural resources, when defined in terms of their general functions (e.g., energy), have increased dramatically over time. The first is that when supplies get tighter, prices go higher and, as a result, there are stronger financial incentives for producers to seek and develop new supplies. The second is that these price stimuli also encourage the development of new technologies designed either to permit more efficient use of existing economic resources or the use of previously unusable resources. The two examples which follow illustrate instances in which the net effect of these two complementary phenomena have multiplied severalfold known economic supplies of specific energy resources.

Over the 25 years between 1944 and 1969, annual world consumption of crude oil rose roughly six times.[9] Because the demand for oil was rising, producers found it profitable to search for and develop new sources of supply in such diverse places as offshore California and the Gulf of Mexico, North and West Africa, northern Alaska and Canada, and the North Sea. They also continued to search for more oil in places (especially the Persian Gulf) where it had previously been discovered. The magnitude of their success in finding new oil supplies is shown by the fact that between 1944 and 1969 total world economic reserves of crude oil rose roughly 12 times.[10] This means that new reserves were accumulating roughly twice as fast as the rise in oil consumption. Of course, this historical experience may not be repeated in the future. Nevertheless, it certainly suggests that, contrary to their assertions, the authors of *The Limits to Growth* were not being overly generous in assuming that between now and 2100, known economic reserves of energy resources would increase only five times.

But what will happen when new reserves of crude oil are no longer found in amounts sufficient to satisfy ever-growing consumption? Then prices will rise and investors will have stronger incentives to develop alternative energy sources. In the Western Hemisphere the two most likely alternative petroleum sources appear to be the oil shale deposits in Colorado, Utah, and Wyoming, and the tar sand deposits in Canada, Colombia, and Venezuela. Recent extimates are that the largest American shale deposit contains about 1.8 trillion barrels of oil. The Canadian and Venezuelan tar sand deposits are each thought to contain about

600 billion barrels, and the Colombian tar sands may contain another one trillion barrels.[11] The petroleum potential of these sources is roughly 46 times larger than the Western Hemisphere's proved reserves (as of 1971) of crude oil and roughly 570 times larger than the Western Hemisphere's total 1971 consumption.[12]

Earth's remaining supplies of known petroleum energy are enormous and still growing. Even if consumption continues to grow at current rates, physical supplies will almost certainly be sufficient to satisfy all demands for at least 200 years. If prices rise and the rate of growth in energy demand slackens, the day of reckoning will be delayed much longer. Nevertheless, unless alternative energy supplies are developed in the interim, at some distant date worldwide physical shortages of petroleum and other fossil fuels will be a real and growing problem. Fortunately, it now seems likely that long before this date virtually unlimited supplies of nuclear fusion power will be available.

The basic technology for a controlled nuclear fusion reaction is presently unknown. Even though many experts would argue that its discovery is imminent (i.e., within 10 years), it would be presumptuous to outline in precise terms just how the nuclear power industry is likely to evolve over the next 100 years. Nevertheless, some idea of the likely significance of this energy source can be inferred from past experiences with fundamental energy technology breakthroughs. Thus our second example is the rather hoary one of the ultimately successful 250-year search by English pig iron producers for cheaper fuel.

Pig iron was initially made by heating iron ore with charcoal. Charcoal was made from timber—a stand of 3000 acres being necessary to provide sufficient charcoal for smelting only 1000 tons.[13] By the beginning of the reign of Elizabeth I (1558), the pig iron industry's growth had so depleted England's timber reserves that it was recognized as a serious national problem.

Higher charcoal prices were a direct consequence of England's growing timber shortage. In turn, this led to a rise in the production costs of the English ironmasters and, as a result, England became a net importer of pig iron from countries (principally Sweden) with more abundant timber reserves. Because the English ironmasters recognized that their profits would rise if fuel costs were lowered, many attempted to substitute cheap coal for expensive charcoal. None succeeded until 1709, when Abraham Darby proved the technological feasibility of using coke, a coal derivative. However, the quality of coke-made pig iron was so bad that it was unacceptable for anything but the crudest pig iron castings. Thus, English timber became progressively scarcer.

Between 1750 and 1780 minor technological innovations gradually raised the quality of coke-made pig iron. For this reason, during these 30 years many English ironmasters decided that it was now profitable to switch from charcoal to coke: The quality of coke-made pig iron had now risen enough that its lower quality was more than offset by its lower cost. Nevertheless, England continued to import Swedish pig iron, and no other country followed her switch to coke. Indeed, charcoal continued to be used in northwestern England where timber remained relatively abundant. These facts imply that in these other pig iron producing regions the lower cost of coal failed to offset the lower quality of the pig iron made from it—no doubt because, in the more heavily forested areas, timber was not in such short supply and therefore its price had not risen high enough to make this switch profitable.

In the last quarter of the eighteenth century a series of major English innovations in pig iron production (especially puddling) raised the quality of coke-made pig iron dramatically. For most purposes the significance of the quality differential between coke-made and charcoal-made pig iron simply disappeared. As a consequence, there was a rapid change in the status of the English iron industry: England was no longer a high-cost marginal producer; instead, its huge reserves of high-quality coking coal (with a Btu content many thousand times larger than its timber reserves) enabled it to become the world's lowest cost pig iron producer. In turn, this meant that the date when the Malthusian apocalypse would have threatened the English iron industry was delayed several hundred years.

The charcoal-coke example illustrates how scarcity and technology continuously interact to increase the economic stocks of what are, in a physical sense, finite stocks of resources. One hypothetical permutation of this example will illustrate the real importance of these scarcity-induced technological innovations even more precisely. The U.S. (excluding interior Alaska) contains roughly 600 million acres of forest land. Suppose the technology making possible the use of coking coal had never been perfected and the thermal efficiency of the charcoal process had remained at its 1750 level. Then, after just two years at current (i.e., 1973) levels of production, the ravenous charcoal appetite of the American pig iron producers could be satisfied only by leveling all of these forests. Can there be any doubt that, in the absence of innovations that multiplied many thousandfold the economical fuel supplies, pig iron would cost many times more than it currently does, and that demand would therefore be far less?

The charcoal-coke example illustrates an actual instance of a fundamental technological breakthrough effectively leading to an enormous increase in the economic stocks of Earth's energy resources. Presently, nuclear fusion holds similar promise. If this promise is realized, Earth's residents need never fear the physical exhaustion of their energy supplies. In view of Earth's huge and still growing net reserves of economical fossil fuel energies and the informed judgment that a commercial fusion process is likely to be feasible within 100 years, it is clear that the Malthusian spectre should have almost no influence on U.S. energy policy at this time.[14] Of course, if nuclear fusion or some other fossil fuel substitute (e.g., solar energy) appears to be no closer to commercial production 50 to 100 years from now, this conclusion will have to be reconsidered.

PARADOX: POSSIBLE ENERGY SHORTAGES AT ANY TIME DURING THE NEXT 15 TO 30 YEARS

Because the reports of the imminent exhaustion of Earth's energy resources have been greatly exaggerated, our energy policymakers should not be concerned with the "limit to growth" problem at this time. Does this mean that the U.S. should not be concerned about obtaining adequate energy supplies? That no national energy policy is needed? Unfortunately, these questions de-

Table 1-2 Crude Oil Consumption and Reserves

Country/Area	Crude Oil Consumption in 1971 [a] (billion barrels)	Proved Crude Oil Reserves 1/1/73 [b] (billion barrels)	Ratio of Crude Oil Reserves to Crude Oil Consumption
United States	5.24	36.82	7.03
Western Europe	4.78	8.58	1.79
U.S.S.R., E. Europe, and China	2.67	98.0	36.7
Japan	1.61	0.0	0.0
Other Western Hemisphere	1.65	42.81	26.0
Other Eastern Hemisphere	1.61	462.25	288.3

SOURCES: [a] British Petroleum, *BP Statistical Review of the World Oil Industry, 1971*, p. 20.
[b] *Oil and Gas Journal* (December 25, 1972), pp. 82–83.

serve negative answers because there is presently a high probability of severe energy shortages at any time during the next 15 to 30 years. No doubt this statement sounds paradoxical: If Earth possesses adequate petroleum reserves to supply all demands for at least 100 years, how can severe shortages be possible in the near future? The key to understanding this paradox is provided by the fact that while our planet is known to contain huge and growing reserves of low-cost petroleum, the U.S. and most of the major non-Communist petroleum-consuming countries do not (Table 1-2). Already they rely on imports to supply a large fraction of their oil needs (Table 1-3). The oil import dependence of Western Europe and Japan is so extensive that it cannot get appreciably worse.[15] But, barring offsetting policies, the U.S. reliance on oil imports should rise sharply (Table 1-4). The principal cause of our rising reliance is that while the United States' annual energy demand will roughly double by the decade 1985–1995, over the same period our annual production of both natural gas (whose sale is already heavily rationed) and crude oil is not expected to rise much above current levels.[16] Because expanded output of the other two large (or potentially large) and presently economical near-term domestic power sources—coal and nuclear (fission) power—is being delayed by environmental restraints and technical difficulties, it is inevitable that the U.S. will become much more depen-

Table 1-3 Net Oil Imports During 1971

Country/Area	Net Oil Imports (billion barrels) [a]	Ratio of Net Imports to Total Consumption
United States	1.37	0.24
Western Europe	4.67	0.95
U.S.S.R., E. Europe	−0.37	Net exporter
Japan	1.61	1.00
Other Western Hemisphere	−0.88	Net exporter
Other Eastern Hemisphere	−6.20	Net exporter
Measurement Error	−0.20	—

[a] SOURCE: British Petroleum, *BP Statistical Review of the World Oil Industry, 1971*, p. 10.

Table 1-4 U.S. Oil and Natural Gas Imports

	1970	1975 [a]	1980 [a]	1985 [a]
Oil imports				
Million barrels per day	3.4	7.3	10.7	14.8
(percentage of total U.S. oil consumption)	(22)	(41)	(49)	(57)
Natural gas imports				
Trillion cubic feet	0.9	1.6	3.8	6.8
(percentage of total U.S. gas consumption)	(4)	(7)	(17)	(28)
Oil and natural gas imports				
Quadrillion Btu	8.4	17.2	26.9	37.2
(percentage of total U.S. energy consumption)	(12)	(21)	(26)	(30)

SOURCE: National Petroleum Council, *U.S. Energy Outlook: An Initial Appraisal, 1971–1985*, Vol. 2, pp. XXVII–XXXIV.

[a] Estimated figures.

dent on oil and gas imports. If this flow of imports should be interrupted, the U.S. would face severe energy shortages until alternative supplies could be developed or steps were taken to reduce demand. This could take several years. During the interim, the cost to the economy would be very high because of the absence of short run substitutes; even after the short run shortage was over, costs would continue higher because the newly developed energy supplies would be more expensive. In the absence of effective countervailing policies, interruptions of oil imports must be regarded as a real possibility (chapter 2). In view of their potential high cost, this is a possibility the U.S. should insure against.

2.

THE SECURITY OF
U.S. OIL AND GAS
SUPPLIES

Imports of "low-cost" Persian Gulf crude oil began to trickle into the United States in the early 1950s. An argument with a now familiar ring accompanied these first Middle Eastern imports: Because the flow of oil imports might be interrupted and the economic havoc created by such interruptions would be enormous, the United States should adopt policies designed either to limit its dependence on oil imports or to create ready reserves. Besides justifying oil import quotas, this argument soon provided the principal rationale for such seemingly contradictory policies as depletion allowances aimed at encouraging higher domestic production of oil and gas and market demand prorationing aimed at restricting domestic oil and gas production and thereby creating "emergency" spare capacity.

At least until the mid-1960s, the national security justification for oil and gas policies had a noticeably false ring. The U.S. imported relatively small quantities of oil and gas, and virtually all of this came from what were militarily and politically secure Caribbean or Canadian sources. Prolonged interruptions from either source were unlikely. Moreover, even if they did occur, the U.S. had ample reserves of readily developable domestic supplies.

However, because of rapidly changed conditions from the early 1960s to the present, the national security argument tolls much truer today. The United States depended on oil imports to provide more than 30 percent of its petroleum needs in 1973; Interior Department projections (cited in chapter 1) point to imports having to satisfy 60 percent of our crude oil demands between 1980 and 1985. The U.S. now has run out of readily available spare energy capacity, and even with a crash program it will take until the late 1970s before large new supplies (from any domestic source) can be developed. Thus, a sudden interruption of oil imports would require severe rationing throughout the American economy. Preventing such interruptions or minimizing the costs (including the need to respond with military force), if they occur, has been proclaimed as the chief goal of many of the United States' oil and gas policies. The case studies in Part II explain why our energy policies failed to achieve this goal. This chapter addresses a much more fundamental issue: the threat that oil import interruptions pose to the United States.

SOURCES AND COSTS OF U.S. OIL IMPORTS

Crude oil reservoirs located in different parts of the world show dramatic differences in size and productivity. These fortuitous geologic differences give rise to huge regional differences both in production costs (see chapter 4) and the speed with which output can be expanded. To illustrate, by far the largest and most productive crude oil sources are located near the Persian Gulf. This region is pocketed with multibillion barrel oil fields, with the "typical" well producing several thousand barrels daily. Because of the abundance of easily accessible resources, Persian Gulf crude currently costs roughly 10 cents per barrel to produce.[1] Recent experience and engineering data both indicate that output from any of the large Persian Gulf sources could easily be doubled or even tripled within just a few years and with no appreciable rise in unit production costs. In contrast, large quantities of American oil cost more than $3.00 per barrel to produce because it comes from small fields with wells capable of producing only two to five barrels per day.[2] Moreover, unless the price for U.S.-produced crude oil rises sharply, domestic output probably cannot be raised much above current levels.[3] Even if such a price rise occurred, because of the huge number of additional wells required it would be several years before domestic output would rise appreciably.

The U.S. imports oil because, even after including production taxes (i.e., royalties paid to the country in which the oil is produced) and transportation costs, it is cheaper than much of the oil that can be produced domestically. Table 2-1 shows the sources of U.S. oil imports in 1971. Western Hemisphere sources were still supplying 78 percent of the total. Table 2-2 shows the Interior Department's most recent projections (January 1973) of the sources of U.S. oil imports in 1975, 1980, and 1985. These indicate that the Persian Gulf states (especially Iran and Saudi Arabia) will soon become the predominant source of the United States' oil imports. The Interior Department bases these projections on its assessment that the "major world supply areas, with the exception of the Middle East, may be considered [to be operating] at maximum levels." [4]

All import projections should be regarded as highly speculative. Historically, unanticipated changes in the United States' future oil demands or the unexpected development (or lack of development) of new domestic or foreign supplies have dated such projections very quickly. For example, the oil import projections made by a presidential cabinet task force in 1970 were dated within the year.[5] Three causes of their speedy obsolescence were (1) unanticipated delays in building the trans-Alaskan pipeline, (2) higher oil demands because of growing natural gas shortages, and (3) higher oil demands as a result of recent pollution control measures. Nevertheless, sharply higher American imports of Persian Gulf oil seem certain over the next few years.

Although Persian Gulf oil costs roughly 10 cents per barrel to produce, it was selling for about $8.00 per barrel at Persian Gulf ports in late 1973.[6] In view of the fact that, relative to current and anticipated world demand for the next 15 to 30 years, known reserves of readily developable low-cost oil are enormous (Table 2-3), this huge differential between prices and costs must be attributed to the success of an immensely powerful monopoly. It is

Table 2-1 Sources of U.S. Imports of Crude Oil and Products, 1971

Source Country	Total Crude Oil and Products Imports (000 barrels daily)	Percent of Total
Western Hemisphere		
Venezuela	998.2	25.8
Canada	858.0	22.1
Netherland West Indies	416.7	10.7
Virgin Islands	270.0	7.0
Trinidad and Tobago	175.8	4.5
Bahama Islands	149.5	3.9
Puerto Rico	95.3	2.4
Other	68.5	2.2
Total Western Hemisphere	3032.0	78.2
Eastern Hemisphere		
North Africa		
Libya	54.0	1.4
Egypt	19.0	0.5
Algeria	13.7	0.4
West Africa		
Nigeria	99.4	2.7
Middle East (Persian Gulf)		
Saudi Arabia	130.5	3.4
Iran	114.8	3.0
Abu Dhabi	79.5	2.0
Kuwait	36.6	1.0
Iraq	10.8	0.3
Bahrain	10.4	0.3
Far East		
Indonesia	110.2	2.8
Other	165.5	4.3
Total Eastern Hemisphere	844.4	21.8
Grand Total	3876.4	100.0

SOURCE: United States Department of Interior, "Detailed Responses to Questions Posed by the Committee on Interior and Insular Affairs," United States Senate (January 1973), Table 4-2.

the actions of that monopoly, the Organization of Petroleum Exporting Countries (OPEC), which provide the chief threat to the security of U.S. oil supplies.

THREATS TO U.S. OIL SUPPLIES

Does the threat of oil import interruptions constitute a real danger to the United States—a danger justifying the adoption of costly preventive policies? In order to answer this question, we need at least a qualitative idea of the probability of an oil import interruption and the likely costs of such an occurrence.

Wars Involving the U.S. as a Participant

A recent Cabinet-level review of U.S. oil import policy concluded that the consequence of oil import interruptions from wars in which the United States is a direct participant can be dismissed as being of little real significance. Three persuasive reasons were offered for this conslusion: (1) "Experience . . . in Korea and Vietnam indicates that dependence on foreign oil supplies in limited wars does not lead to protracted supply interruptions." [7] (2) "If [a nuclear war] did occur, the continuity of oil supply would not likely be a matter of major significance." [8] (3) A "general non-nuclear war is considered unlikely." However, if there were such a war and U.S. security were directly threatened because of resultant oil shortages, then "the question would be how long that war could continue without either settlement or escalation into a nuclear exchange." [9] In sum, if—as a result of its being at war—U.S. oil imports are interrupted, the additional costs directly attributable to such interruption would be slight. Thus, even if U.S. involvement in wars is likely (and the post-Vietnam Nixon Administration would deny this), it cannot justify preventive policies costing several billion dollars annually.

Regional Wars Involving Large Oil Exporters

With the important exception of Iran, all of the Persian Gulf countries are Arab. The continuing hostility between most Arab states and Israel raises the spectre of regional wars interrupting the

Table 2-2 United States Estimated Oil Imports
U.S. Interior Department's Case III

Source	1975		1980		1985	
	Thousand Barrels Daily	Percent Total	Thousand Barrels Daily	Percent Total	Thousand Barrels Daily	Percent Total
Canada	1,275	15.0	1,925	18.1	2,750	20.4
Caribbean	1,550	18.2	1,500	14.1	1,500	11.1
Other Western Hemisphere	1,190	14.0	1,600	15.1	2,000	14.8
Non-Communist Europe	155	1.8	180	1.7	200	1.5
Africa	400	4.7	800	7.5	1,200	8.9
Middle East	3,744	44.0	4,349	40.9	5,449	40.5
Far East	175	2.1	250	2.4	350	2.6
Soviet Bloc	15	0.2	20	0.2	25	0.2
Total	8,504	100.0	10,624	100.0	13,474	100.0
Percent of total required supply	46.6		47.6		52.2	

U.S. Interior Department's Case IV

Source	1975		1980		1985	
	Thousand Barrels Daily	Percent Total	Thousand Barrels Daily	Percent Total	Thousand Barrels Daily	Percent Total
Canada	1,275	13.2	1,925	11.7	2,750	14.3
Caribbean	1,550	16.0	1,500	9.1	1,500	7.8
Other Western Hemisphere	1,190	12.3	1,600	9.8	2,000	10.4
Non-Communist Europe	155	1.6	180	1.1	200	1.0
Africa	400	4.1	800	4.9	1,200	6.3
Middle East	4,918	50.8	10,130	61.8	11,223	58.3
Far East	175	1.8	250	1.5	350	1.8
Soviet Bloc	15	0.2	20	0.1	25	0.1
Total	9,678	100.0	16,405	100.0	19,248	100.0
Percent of total required supply	50.1		64.8		64.7	

SOURCE: United States Department of Interior, "Detailed Responses to Questions Posed by the Committee on Interior and Insular Affairs," United States Senate (January 1973), Table 4-1.

Table 2-3 Nations with Proved Crude Oil Reserves of at Least 1 Billion Barrels, 1973

Source Country	Proved Crude Oil Reserves 1/1/73 (billion barrels)	Estimated 1972 Crude Oil (000 barrels daily)	Ratio of Annual Crude Oil Output to Currently Proved Reserves
Asia Pacific			
Australia	2.1	308.0	0.0535
Brunei-Malaysia	1.5	278.0	0.0676
Indonesia	10.0	1027.0	0.0375
Other	1.3	200.6	0.0563
Europe			
Norway	2.0	34.0	0.0062
United Kingdom	5.0	2.0	0.0001
Yugoslavia	3.5	59.0	0.0061
Other	1.6	272.0	0.0621
Middle East			
Abu Dhabi	20.8	1,000.0	0.0175
Dubai	2.0	130.0	0.0237
Iran	65.0	4,900.0	0.0275
Iraq	29.0	1,500.0	0.0189
Kuwait	64.9	2,750.0	0.0155
Neutral Zone	16.0	545.0	0.0124
Oman	5.0	280.0	0.0204
Qatar	7.0	450.0	0.0235
Saudi Arabia	138.0	5,255.0	0.0139
Syria	7.3	120.0	0.0060
Other	0.9	257.0	0.1042

Africa			
Algeria	47.0	1,061.0	0.0082
Angola	1.2	135.0	0.0411
Congo-Brazzaville	5.0	7.5	0.0005
Egypt	5.2	227.0	0.0159
Libya	30.4	2,230.0	0.0268
Nigeria	15.0	1,800.0	0.0438
Tunisia	1.0	80.0	0.0292
Other	1.6	125.0	0.0285
Western Hemisphere			
Argentina	4.9	435.0	0.0324
Canada	10.2	1,490.0	0.0533
Columbia	1.5	192.0	0.0467
Ecuador	5.8	59.4	0.0037
Trinidad-Tobago	2.0	143.0	0.0261
United States	36.8	9,500.0	0.0942
Venezuela	13.7	3,200.0	0.0853
Other	2.7	295.1	0.0400
Total Non-Communist Nations	566.9	40,347.6	0.0260

SOURCE: "Worldwide Oil at a Glance," *Oil and Gas Journal* (December 25, 1972), pp. 82–83.

flow of Persian Gulf oil at any time. Indeed, at this writing (November 1973), there is worldwide panic because the Arab states have cut oil exports by roughly 25 percent in an attempt to force the major oil-consuming countries to adopt anti-Israeli foreign policies. Current reaction to an interruption of this magnitude may be exaggerated. Nevertheless, as long as the Mideast remains so politically volatile, policies aimed at reducing dependence on this oil are desirable.

The OPEC Oil Monopoly

Since the early 1950s, crude oil produced in the major oil-exporting countries has always sold at a price many times greater than its cost. Because, relative to current and projected levels of demand, there are huge quantities of low-cost oil, these profits must be attributed to the successful exercise of monopoly power. Specifically, whenever a product's price exceeds the cost of producing an additional unit, producers will find it profitable to produce and sell that unit. Unfortunately for them, if each producer follows what he perceives to be his self-interest and produces all units for which price exceeds cost, industry output will expand, causing prices to fall and profits to dwindle. The price fall will stop only when the profit incentive to expand output ceases. This level of output will be reached only when price equals the costs of producing extra units.

The process just described is called competition. Realizing that the ultimate result of competition is lower profits for every firm in the industry, producers of almost any product desire to avoid it. To do so each must act to limit his sales. Each will do so only if he has good reason for expecting that his competitors will do likewise. Monopoly power is being exercised when the members of an industry are successful in reducing their output and thereby keeping their product's price higher than the cost of producing additional units. Enforcement of monopoly control typically becomes more difficult the greater the differential between prices and costs because this strengthens each firm's incentive to "cheat" and raise its profits by raising sales.

Monopoly power is likely to be stronger the fewer the number

of firms presently in or likely to soon enter an industry, the easier⚹
collusion is, and the less aggressive the industry's customers are ⚹
when searching for lower-priced alternatives. In his brilliant study
of the world petroleum market, M. A. Adelman shows how these
factors were interacting throughout the 1950s to give the international petroleum industry considerable monopoly power.[10] Nevertheless, by the late 1950s the difference between prices and costs
was so enormous that "cheating" had become widespread: sales
of Persian Gulf oil expanded and prices began to fall. These falling
prices led directly to the formation of OPEC—a cartel composed
of the leading oil-exporting nations, committed to stabilizing and,
later, raising prices.

In return for permission to produce and sell a nation's oil, the
international oil companies pay royalties (on each barrel sold) to
the host government. These royalties—which are some large fraction of the crude oil's posted price—comprise the bulk of each
producing country's share of the profits from the sale of its oil.
Because of price-cutting, crude oil prices had fallen below the
posted price in 1959. Believing that under the circumstances their
royalty payments to the host countries should be reduced, the international oil companies cut the posted price. Because the price
fall continued, they cut the posted price a second time in 1960.

Because lower posted prices meant lower royalties, the oil-exporting nations were incensed at the internationals' "arbitrary" action. Representatives of five of these countries (Iraq, Iran, Kuwait,
Saudi Arabia, and Venezuela), which together supplied 80 percent
of the oil entering world trade, met at Baghdad to consider ways to
stop and, if possible, reverse the "unfair" erosion of their monopoly profits. They agreed to establish OPEC, with the initial goal of
restoring prices to pre-cut levels. Thus, OPEC's charter said:

> That members shall study and formulate a system to ensure the stabili-
> zation of prices by, among other means, the regulation of production,
> with due regard to the interests of the producing and the consuming na-
> tions, and to the necessity of securing a steady income to the producing
> countries . . . [and] . . . if . . . as a result of the application of any
> unanimous decision of this Conference any sanctions are employed, di-
> rectly or indirectly, by any interested Company against one or more of

the Member Countries, no other Member shall accept any offer of beneficial treatment, whether in the form of an increase in exports or any improvement in prices, which may be made to it by any such Company or Companies with the intention of discouraging the application of the unanimous decision reached by the conference.[11]

With the exception of Canada, all of the major oil-exporting nations soon joined the OPEC cartel.[12] Nevertheless, it failed to achieve its stated goal; the trend for crude oil prices was downward throughout the 1960s.[13] However, because these prices were still many times greater than costs, this is not evidence that OPEC actually failed. Indeed, when compared with past cartels, its success at preventing much more dramatic price cuts distinguishes it as having been quite successful.[14]

In the early 1970s OPEC suddenly became much more successful—crude oil prices actually began to rise sharply even though the already low production costs remained steady or fell. M. A. Adelman argues that OPEC's recent successes should be attributed in large part to misguided policies of the U.S. State Department. His damning indictment is so persuasive that it merits extensive quotation. Adelman writes:

In May 1970 the trans-Arabian pipeline was blocked by Syria to obtain higher payments for the transit rights, while the Libyan government began to impose production cutbacks on most of the companies operating there, to force them to agree to higher taxes. Although the direct effect of the cutback and closure was small, the effect on tanker rates was spectacular, and product prices and profits shot up.

The companies producing in Libya speedily agreed to a tax increase. The Persian Gulf producing countries then demanded and received the same increase, whereupon Libya demanded a further increase and the Persian Gulf countries followed suit. Finally, agreements were signed at Teheran in February 1971, increasing tax and royalty payments at the Persian Gulf as of June 1971 by about 47 cents per barrel, and rising to about 66 cents in 1975. North African and Nigerian increases were larger. In Venezuela the previous 1966 agreement was disregarded and higher taxes were simply legislated. . . .

Without active support from the United States, OPEC might never have achieved much. When the first Libyan cutbacks were decreed in

May 1970, the United States could have easily convened the oil companies to work out an insurance scheme whereby any single company forced to shut down would have crude oil supplied by the others. . . . Had that been done, all companies might have been shut down, and the Libyan government would have lost all production income. It would have been helpful but not necessary to freeze its deposits abroad. The OPEC nations were unprepared for conflict. Their unity would have been severely tested and probably destroyed. The revenue losses of Libya would have been gains to all other producing nations, and all would have realized the danger of trying to pressure the consuming countries. . . .

. . . A month after the November agreements with Libya, a special OPEC meeting in Caracas first resolved on "concrete and simultaneous action," but this had not been explained or translated into a threat of cutoff even as late as January 13, nor by January 16, when the companies submitted their proposals for higher and escalating taxes.

Then came the turning point: The United States convened a meeting in Paris of the OECD nations [countries belonging to the Organization for Economic Cooperation and Development account for most oil consumption] on January 20. . . . The OECD meeting could have kept silent, thereby keeping the OPEC nations guessing, and moderating their demands for fear of counteraction. Or they might have told the press they were sure the OPEC nations were too mature and statesmanlike to do anything drastic, because after all the OECD nations had some drastic options open to them too . . . but why inflame opinion by talking about those things? Instead an OECD spokesman praised the companies' offer, and declined to estimate its cost to the consuming countries. He stated that the meeting had not discussed "contingency arrangements for coping with an oil shortage." This was an advance capitulation. The OPEC nations now had a signal to go full speed ahead because there would be no resistance.

Before January 20, an open threat by the OPEC nations would not have been credible, in view of the previous failure of even mild attempts at production regulation in 1965 and 1966. But after the capitulation, threats were credible and were made often. . . . They culminated in a resolution passed on February 7 by nine OPEC members, including Venezuela but not Indonesia, providing for an embargo after two weeks if their demands were not met. The Iranian Finance Minister, chief of the producing nations' team, said: "There is no question of negotiations or resuming negotiations. It's just the acceptance of our terms." . . .

The United States had been active in the meantime. Our Under Secretary of State arrived in Tehran January 17, publicly stating his government's interest in "stable and predictable" prices, which in context meant higher prices. He told the Shah of Iran the damage that would be done to Europe and Japan if oil supplies were cut off. Perhaps this is why the Shah soon thereafter made the first threat to cut off supply.

Resistance to the OPEC demands would have shattered the nascent cartel. As late as January 24, the Shah told the press: "If the oil producing countries suffer even the slightest defeat, it would be the death-knell for OPEC, and from then on the countries would no longer have the courage to get together." . . .

The oil companies knew better than to take the "agreements" seriously; they had been there before. . . . This was borne out in August of 1971. . . . The OPEC governments made their demands. The companies made their offer. The governments refused it and broke off the talks. The companies made a better offer, taxes were raised again, and crude oil prices with them. . . .

There has been unparalleled turbulence since the State Department special conference. . . . The genie is out of the bottle. The OPEC nations have had a great success with the threat of embargo and will not put the weapon away. The turbulence will continue as taxes and prices are raised again and again.[15]

Whatever the reasons, OPEC has become one of the most successful cartels in history. Adelman calculated that its members collected $15 billion in monopoly profits during 1972; moreover, if late-1973 world prices hold, their annual profits could exceed $60 billion in 1974.[16]

POLITICS AND GREED

The OPEC nations have reaped tremendous economic and political gains from their recent successful threats to embargo oil sales. Besides soaring oil profits, they have demonstrated that they can virtually dictate to the wealthy Western oil-consuming nations— many of whom were once their colonialist "oppressors"—the terms at which they are willing to sell. Future threats seem inevitable. This poses a cruel dilemma for the oil-consuming nations: If they succumb to threats of embargo, they face ever-rising energy prices and, because the OPEC countries will grow even more powerful, continued rapid erosion of their oil security. If they resist these threats, they face a lengthy and extremely costly oil embargo.[17] The leading OPEC nations possess huge and ever-growing foreign exchange reserves. They believe (correctly) that they are far better prepared to bear the costs of a lengthy embargo than are their prosperous but oil-short and, in the short run, oil-dependent customers. Moreover, an embargo would be necessary only because the large oil-consuming nations had refused to pay a "fair" price for crude oil.

OTHER FACTORS AFFECTING THE SECURITY OF FUTURE U.S. PETROLEUM SUPPLIES

Europe's Emergence as a Large Oil Producer

In mid-May 1970, a consortium of oil companies announced discovery of the 7-billion-barrel East Ekofisk oil field in the North Sea. They also announced that East Ekofisk crude was high quality and the discovery well could produce at least 10,000 barrels of oil per day.[18] The combination of these four factors—a large quantity of oil, high output per well, high quality, and proximity to European markets—guaranteed that huge profits would be reaped from this oil's sale.

In the article announcing the Ekofisk discovery, *The Oil and Gas Journal* wrote:

Based on . . . experience of the past 5 years . . . some operators, steeped in disappointment, have pulled in their horns, cut their budgets and staffs, and expressed little interest in further North Sea ventures.

Now this will all change. A bright new era lies in store for the North Sea and for Europe. Seismic surveys will be restudied, new ones made, and offshore rigs will descend on the sea in unprecedented numbers as operating groups pursue an entirely new target—Tertiary oil. And *big* oil.[19]

These optimistic expectations of other large North Sea finds were soon confirmed. In 1972 alone, at least 13 new oil fields were discovered; most will prove commercial.[20] At the end of 1972, industry sources were saying that ultimately recoverable reserves of

North Sea crude oil would be 42 billion barrels.[21] If past experience with industry estimates offers any guide, this estimate will be revised sharply upward over the next few years.

North Sea crude oil output will be inconsequential until completion of the pipelines necessary for shipping large quantities of oil from the wellheads to waiting coastal refineries. However, by 1975, when pipelines from just two of the fields—East Ekofisk and Forties—have been completed, the North Sea's daily output should be at least 700,000 barrels. Thereafter output will grow rapidly as other large fields come on stream. Estimates of daily output well in excess of 4 million barrels during the early 1980s are now circulating in Europe.[22] If North Sea output does reach these levels, Western Europe's dependence on OPEC oil will be reduced to between 50 and 80 percent of its total demand. Other things being equal, this should help to reduce the monopoly power possessed by that cartel and this, in turn, should reduce the magnitude of the United States' oil security problems.

Oil and Israel

Many foreign policy experts question the desirability of the U.S. maintaining its present strategic commitments to Israel because OPEC's Arab members have reacted to these commitments by interrupting oil exports. Those advancing this argument are implicitly suggesting that the U.S. could virtually eliminate OPEC's threats to its oil security by severing most ties with Israel. Is this a valid conclusion?

Suppose the U.S. did curtail its strategic commitments to Israel because it wished to persuade some OPEC members to ameliorate other onerous demands. Since such a move would only be made under duress, both our allies and enemies would regard it as positive affirmation of the oil cartel's enormous monopoly power. The principal consequence of this affirmation would almost certainly be a further rise in OPEC's monopoly power and, thus, further erosion of U.S. oil security. In addition to creating a climate more favorable to additional crude oil price rises, this might also encourage non-Arab OPEC members to issue similar threats aimed at achieving political goals in other parts of the world. In sum, reduction of threats to our oil security is not likely to be a consequence of a diminished level of commitments to Israel.

Oil Imports and the Balance of Payments

As a result of our increased imports of more expensive OPEC oil, these countries are enjoying rapidly growing revenues. Many believe that this poses a threat to the security of the United States distinguishable from the threat to shut off our access to OPEC supplies. In its most simplistic form their argument goes: Some OPEC countries will use a large fraction of their oil revenues to accumulate highly liquid dollar hoards. Then, if the U.S. takes steps contrary to their interests, they will counterattack by dumping dollars—driving down their price—and thereby disrupting the fragile world monetary system. The chief flaw in this argument is that the U.S. and its principal allies could quickly sterilize the adverse consequences attributable to any predatory financial strategy not also accompanied by a credible threat to foreclose access to OPEC oil. As a first step, the central banks of the non-OPEC countries could simply buy the dumped currency. (Assuming that exchange rates were thought to be near "true" parity prior to any decision to dump dollars, private investors would join in gobbling them up.) In the unlikely event that their currency reserves would be inadequate for this task, the U.S. (i.e., the assumed target country) could always take the dramatic but effective step of freezing all American assets held by the hostile foreign government and its nationals.

Petroleum Imports from the Soviet Union

The Soviet Union may be exporting large quantities of crude oil and natural gas to the United States in the late 1970s. Many Americans oppose our reliance on energy imports from the nation that provides the chief threat to our very existence. This opposition is misplaced. Unlike the OPEC countries, the Soviets already possess a variety of economic, military, and political tools that could be used to force a direct confrontation with the United States. Another tool is redundant. There may come a time when the Soviets choose to halt their oil exports. But this will only be when the combined force of a great many other factors and events causes their leadership to conclude that a confrontation is either desirable or inevitable. In sum, reliance on Soviet oil and gas imports does not pose an additional security threat to the U.S. Thus, other things being equal, the substitution of Soviet petroleum for OPEC petroleum should enhance the United States' security.

CONCLUSION

Through their control of most of the non-Communist reserves of low-cost crude oil, the OPEC countries currently possess the economic and political clout of a major world power. It is no exaggeration to say that they have achieved this high status by blackmailing the oil-short Western consuming nations. Past successes with blackmail virtually guarantee future repetitions. Moreover, if the blackmail demands are not met, an oil embargo is now a very real threat. For these reasons, costly policies are justifiable if they succeed in neutralizing the blackmailers' threats.

3.

POLLUTION

United States energy policymakers are responsible for assuring the availability of huge quantities of energy at lowest cost. Except for products produced by the perfectly competitive firms of textbook fame, successful performance of such a duty is always difficult. This chapter will explain why successful performance of this charge is rendered even more difficult by recent public recognition that environmental pollution is often a by-product of producing, transporting, and consuming energy.

SIMPLE ANALYTICS OF THE
POLLUTION PROBLEM

Pollutants are the socially costly by-products of what would otherwise be socially desirable activities. It follows directly that a reduction in the quantity of pollutants increases society's welfare. Society's justified concern with the pollution problem raises two practical questions: How should a society determine what activities are polluting (i.e., socially undesirable)? Why do individuals and institutions pollute if it is socially undesirable?

An economic activity is polluting whenever society's evaluation of the total cost attributable to it, including the costs of its undesirable by-products, exceeds society's evaluation of the total benefits. In order to evaluate social costs and benefits, every society must decide whose tastes should be considered legitimate and how heavily it should weigh the legitimate tastes of different citizens.[1] The importance of a society's answers to these questions is best illustrated by a recent example.

In order to market the large quantities of crude oil known to be at Prudhoe Bay on the Alaskan North Slope, a consortium of oil companies planned to build a trans-Alaskan pipeline. If only their tastes had been considered, the fact that these oil companies were willing to spend several billion dollars building this pipeline demonstrated conclusively that, in their view, the benefits of this project exceeded its costs. That is, judged from their perspective, this project was not polluting. In contrast, a coalition of environmental groups (including the Wilderness Society and the Friends of Earth) spent large sums opposing construction of this pipeline because, in their view, its social costs far outstripped its social benefits. Suppose the U.S. government had decided that the tastes of only one of these opposing interest groups were legitimate. Then, deciding the desirability of the Alaskan pipeline would have been straightforward. Similarly, even if it decided that both groups' tastes were legitimate, as long as it also decided how heavily each group's tastes should be weighed, it would have had a basis for deciding whether this project should have been undertaken.

Unfortunately, there are no tests that enable our government to objectively decide whose tastes to consider and how heavily to weigh different citizens' tastes. In every instance, society's decisionmakers must premise their answers to these crucially important questions on what is essentially a subjective value judgment. Disputes over the subjectivity of the government's answers to these questions are inevitable; they are likely to prove especially rancorous when the pollution is of an aesthetic nature.

In addition to the necessity of resolving legitimacy questions, attempts to evaluate social costs and benefits are also plagued by the need to prevent the legitimate victims or beneficiaries of any potentially polluting activity from exaggerating the magnitude of its benefits or costs.[2] The Alaskan pipeline controversy also serves to illustrate this problem: Pro-pipeliners inflated its value in enhancing U.S. oil security or in raising the living standards of the native

Americans living near Prudhoe Bay's shores; opponents painted dismal pictures of the "rape" of our last virgin wilderness and of the inevitability of massive oil spills. Such distortions can seriously complicate the problem of "correctly" evaluating the social costs and benefits resulting from any potentially polluting activity.

Until the mid-1960s, pollution control was not an issue that aroused widespread or effective public support. As long as there was public indifference, political leaders tended to resolve the "legitimacy" questions by giving most weight to the interests of those who stood to profit directly from activities which might, as a by-product, damage the environment. This attitude began to change in the 1950s. At least initially however, change proved slow. To illustrate, in response to rising public awareness of the possible damage to health because of air pollution, President Eisenhower said in his 1955 special health message,

> As a result of industrial growth and urban development the atmosphere over some population centers may be approaching the limit of its ability to absorb air pollution with safety to health. I am recommending an increased appropriation to the Public Health Service for studies seeking scientific data and more effective methods of control. [3]

Congress responded to the President's request by passing "an Act to provide research and technical assistance relating to air pollution." [4] An annual appropriation of not more than $5 million (for a period of five years) was provided.

The 1955 air pollution control act was intended to be a limited and strictly construed response to the general problem of air pollution. Even though there was ample evidence that automobiles and stationary power sources contributed to this problem, no mention of any particular form of air pollution was made nor was any particular source singled out for special investigation. Also, the problem was defined by Congress as one of local or regional concern. The committee report recognized

> . . . that it is the primary responsibility of state and local governments to prevent air pollution. The bill does not propose any exercise of police power by the Federal Government and no provisions in it invade the sov-

ereignty of states, counties, or cities. There is no attempt to impose standards of purity.[5]

The automobile was not singled out as a major polluter for two reasons. First, although the 1955 Act was passed partially in response to an increased public awareness of the presence and dangers of air pollution, a sizeable majority of the public apparently failed to realize that exhaust from their own cars could be contributing to the problem. As one observer noted,

In general, the public has only a hazy impression of its own contribution to air pollution. It is difficult to equate a thousand home chimneys or a hundred thousand auto exhaust pipes with a few big, belching smokestacks. The result is that industry is under constant public pressure to reduce the amount of pollution in the sky while those applying the pressure do little or nothing about correcting their own faults.[6]

Secondly, it was feared that if consumers knew that the ordinary family car was a major cause of air pollution, many would be unwilling to bear the cost of controlling the offending emissions. There was "no assurance that the public will ever be willing to pay out of its own pocket for cleaner air" or that the public could be coerced or persuaded into spending "an estimated $30 per family automobile as a highly personalized contribution to air pollution control."[7]

Beginning in the mid-1960s, there was a dramatic change in the American public's perception of the magnitude of current pollution problems. Writing in 1970, L. Jaffe, a legal authority observed,

Now we are faced with an environmental crisis. . . . Until recently there had been no organized pressure for environmental control. The political situation has now changed radically. Every politician is now sounding the call for pure air and pure water. The legislative activity is tremendous. There are new mandates and new calls to action. The stage is being set for the real battle to take place.[8]

As a result of the American public's growing awareness of pollution's costs and of the political decision to respond to the growing unrest, there resulted—quite suddenly in the late

1960s—a new resolution of the "legitimacy" questions. Both federal and state governments, acting on behalf of the American people, adopted and began to enforce much stronger antipollution laws. Congressional adoption of the 1970 amendments to the Clean Air Act best illustrates this change. These created the Environmental Protection Agency and established tough mandatory emission standards for many air pollution sources, including the automobile. These amendments were passed because

Traditional economic indices are no longer viewed as the sole measure of progress. We are entering an era in which qualitative values and aesthetic factors are considered as important as material wealth. . . . People are no longer complacent about the quality of their surroundings. . . . A major task which we face in the future is ensuring that those newly formed public values will be recognized and acted upon.[9]

In 1971 it was thought that meeting the emission standards established in the 1970 Clean Air Act might raise the cost of producing each new automobile by $300 to $800; this testifies to the weight our political leaders were attaching to these "newly formed public values."

Suppose our society has somehow made the political decisions (i.e., answered the "legitimacy" questions) necessary to ascertain if a particular activity is polluting. Having done this it constructs a list of those activities it feels should be classified as polluting. This raises a puzzling question: Why do individuals and institutions pollute if it is socially undesirable? [10] Finding the answer to this question ought to help us design better policies for reducing or eliminating pollution.

There are at least three reasons why individuals and institutions pollute. One is that some polluters are perverse. That is, they derive pleasure from performing socially destructive acts. In this case, the very act of polluting is regarded by the polluter as a consumption good. For example, one by-product of a successful arson attempt (or even a false alarm) is the provocation of intense reactions by many other people. The occupants flee the threatened building and the fire department arrives with masses of equipment.

Don't many arsonists engage in this socially destructive activity precisely because they enjoy provoking these reactions by other people?

Inadequate or inaccurate information is a second cause of pollution. More specifically, because of inadequate information, some projects are undertaken which better information would have revealed to be polluting. One example of such unintentional pollution came to light recently when the U.S. government admitted that many houses constructed on foundations made from uranium tailings had dangerously high radiation counts. This pollution was not deliberate. It occurred because it was not known at the time these houses were constructed that the residual radioactivity in uranium tailings was dangerous.

Fortunately, neither perverseness nor ignorance is the cause of most pollution. Rather, it is the result of a discrepancy between "public" and "private" cost evaluations. Specifically, because certain kinds of social costs have not been levied on the firm, it treats them as zero. Then, when it acts to maximize profits, these costs appear as a kind of wild uncontrolled damage to society. To illustrate, sulphur dioxide (SO_2) is a poisonous by-product from burning high sulphur coal or fuel oil. Many power companies using fossil-fuel-fired steam generators discovered that the cheapest way to produce electricity was to burn cheap, high-sulphur fuel and "dump" any SO_2 into the atmosphere. This method was cheapest only because these companies bore none (or very little) of the pollution costs. Instead, they were borne by residents downwind from where the power plant's excrement entered the atmosphere. This pollution would cease if the government changed the "rules of the game" and adopted measures that imposed these costs on the polluter.

Government policymakers may choose among four types of policies for controlling pollution. In principle, all work by internalizing external costs and benefits. One type of policy choice involves amending laws in ways that facilitate a private solution of the underlying externality problem. To illustrate, many property owners frequently have access to the same oil or gas pool.[11] Traditional Anglo-American property law states that the petroleum in such multiownership pools belongs to those who "capture" it by extraction through their wells. Because in-ground oil and gas is under pressure, it migrates to a flowing well. Thus each producer has an incentive to capture as much petroleum as possible before it is captured by another overlying the same field. (Chapter 5 will explain how this externality problem led to overdrilling which, in turn, caused massive physical and environmental waste in Texas and Louisiana during the 1930s.) One way to alleviate this problem would be to pass laws forcing the compulsory unitization of every oil and gas field by requiring the owners of a field to put one decisionmaker in charge of its entire operation. Because this results in the internalization of all costs and benefits, it eliminates the costly tendency to deplete jointly owned oil fields too quickly. Compulsory unitization laws have now been passed by several oil-producing states. Where enforced, these laws have solved the externality problem. Moreover, they achieved this desirable result in a way that requires no direct intervention by the state in the operation of jointly owned oil fields.

A second policy choice requires use of taxes and subsidies to persuade polluters to behave in more socially desirable ways. This is a carrot-and-stick policy: Subsidies are used to "bribe" polluters to reduce their pollution; taxes are used to punish those who pollute. The chief virtues claimed for this policy are its potential for flexibility and the fact that it does not require government involvement in the minutiae of the potential polluters' day-to-day operations. For example, suppose, after studying the problem of SO_2 air pollution, the government concludes that the cost to society is 10 cents for each pound emitted. Then, it could levy an effluent tax of 10 cents per pound on these emissions. Faced with such a tax, SO_2 polluters will search for the cheapest ways to reduce their emissions. They will continue to emit SO_2 only in those instances where the cost of pollution control exceeds the tax.[12] If, in the future, a larger reduction in SO_2 emissions is thought to be desirable, the government has only to raise the level of the effluent tax. In addition to its flexibility and the fact that it frees the government from the responsibility of daily supervision, the tax-subsidy policy permits the government to place the cost of pollution control on any group it desires. The chief flaws in the tax-subsidy policy are that some kinds of taxes may be difficult (hence very costly) to collect, and that the electorate may be unwilling to pay the price necessary to obtain desired modifications in polluters' behavior.

A third policy choice involves passing laws and regulations compelling polluters to behave in socially desirable ways. Mandatory automobile emission standards are an example. Mandatory standards are usually less flexible than taxes or subsidies and require more direct government supervision. They work best when aimed at achieving quite precise goals using well-established means.[13] If the problem is very complex or the technology for solving it remains uncertain, the more flexible tax-subsidy approach is probably preferable.[14]

The final policy option for controlling pollution requires the government to nationalize high-polluting industries and operate them in a way it deems more socially desirable. For example, the U.S. government's decision to establish the Tennessee Valley Authority was at least partially premised on the hope of reducing pollution costs to residents of this region. This rationalization for nationalization is that the government is able to bring to bear the interests of all citizens, not just a few. While it sounds plausible, this rationalization is frequently wrong. Because government enterprises are, in fact, often more insulated from public criticism than their private counterparts, they may tend to be worse polluters. Nevertheless, suppose we accept this rationalization as valid (as in some cases it will be). Then, the decision to have the government operate high-polluting firms or industries must be regarded as the most radical of the pollution-control options because it requires the government to become totally immersed in the business of producing goods or services formerly supplied by private firms. Such a policy is most likely to be successful in those instances where tight public control is needed in order to solve the underlying pollution problem.

ENERGY AND POLLUTION [15]

Energy production and consumption is a major cause of current environmental degradation. As one Senator noted:

> Airborne pollutants, concentration of nuclear wastes, oil spills, thermal pollution from power plants, extensive modifications of the landscape by the increased construction of transmission lines, refineries, pumped storage facilities, and marine transmission facilities are illustrative causes of environmental problems related to energy production and use. [16]

Detailed discussions about both the impact of current energy policies on our environment and, conversely, the impact of current pollution control policies on our energy demand and supply await the case studies in Part II. Here I wish to spotlight briefly my own views about the overall importance of our energy-environmental problems.

Because American energy consumers have not been charged for the environmental damage which has been or will be a by-product of their consumption, they consume more energy than is "socially" desirable. Thus, the government is justified in taking measures to reduce our energy consumption. The important question requiring prompt answer by our policymakers is a quantitative one: How strong should these measures be? My reasons for favoring relatively strong measures to limit our energy consumption are summarized below.

Currently, it is impossible to assess what will be the real importance of our energy-environmental problems. The causes of this uncertainty are of two kinds: technological uncertainty and taste uncertainty. There are two sources of technological uncertainty. The first lies in our present lack of good information about how successful many of our pollution control policies are likely to be. For example, consider the presently unanswered questions: Will someone find a solution to the problem of nuclear waste disposal? Will the automobile companies successfully meet the stringent 1976 mandatory emission standards? And, will further reductions in automobile emission levels be economically feasible? Much better answers to these questions should be available in just a few years.

The second source of technological uncertainty lies in our extremely sketchy understanding of the ultimate ecological consequences of different levels of pollution. We do not know if the pessimists are correct when they assert that if growth in the production of pollutants is not halted there will be fundamental ecological changes—changes that threaten to make human life more difficult, perhaps impossible, to sustain. Must bold steps be taken immediately to reduce current pollution levels and forestall this possibility? As suggested in chapter 1, in the absence of some fairly hard evidence, apocalyptic arguments like those implicit in the above questions are unpersuasive. Costly policy measures cannot be justified by vague feelings that cataclysm is at hand; for such a radical policy prescription, a much higher standard of evidence should be required.[17] Such evidence has not yet been offered. Until it is, I would dismiss this particular rationalization for taking steps to sharply reduce levels of energy production and consumption.

The "apostles of apocalypse" can be faulted because they recommend a very high-cost strategy to deal with what must presently be regarded as an unlikely occurrence: the end of life as we know it unless radical pollution control measures are taken *immediately*. A decision to dismiss this particular rationalization does not imply that we should avoid taking steps to sharply reduce our production of pollutants. It does mean that another justification is needed.

A much better justification for pollution control measures is simply that large elements of the American citizenry now regard pollution as undesirable. The sudden recognition of the pollution problem in the late 1960s had two causes. First, increasing numbers of citizens were becoming aware that higher levels of pollution imposed measurable real costs. Chief among these were damages to health and especially—crass though it be—real property. Secondly, many citizens began to make the aesthetic judgement that higher levels of pollution lower the "quality of life." This may be called the aesthetic pollution problem. Fear of aesthetic pollution explains much of the environmentalists' opposition to such projects as offshore drilling for oil and construction of new refineries and superports. Specifically, they argue that once such projects are undertaken many of the deleterious consequences can never be reversed.

The future importance of the aesthetic pollution problem is, at present, hard to evaluate.[18] The tastes of Americans about pollution are still in a state of flux. As the costs of pollution control measures are better understood, recent concern about this problem may evaporate as quickly as it appeared. If this concern does not disappear (and I hope it does not), a great variety of pollution control policies will be justified. In the light of our present uncertainty about what will be the feasible technological alternatives for reducing pollution and the fact that much of what we regard as aesthetic pollution is both irreversible and a by-product of energy consumption, reduction in energy consumption appears to be one of the most attractive pollution control options currently available.

4.

DISTRIBUTIONAL CONSEQUENCES OF U.S. OIL AND GAS POLICIES

PRIVILEGE: THE FATAL FLAW

Public debates over U.S. oil and gas policies are especially bitter. There is little disagreement as to the goal of most of these policies—solving one or more of the three problems already discussed. Though people's assessments of the importance of these various problems differ, nearly all Americans agree that their alleviation is a desirable goal. There are two causes of this rancor: the realization that current oil and gas policies have frequently failed to achieve their proclaimed goals (the case studies presented in Part II document this failure in excruciating detail) and the realization that our current policies have conferred valuable rights upon special interest groups. Historically the gift of valuable rights, created as a consequence of governmental policies, has been called privilege. Public opposition to the state's granting of privileges has a distinguished history in the United States. It can explain a large part of the Colonists' opposition to the "arbitrary" actions of the British Crown; the success of Andrew Jackson's efforts to slay the congressionally chartered Second Bank of the United States,[1] and the public support afforded the Muckrakers in their turn-of-the-century attack on political corruption.[2] As the following examples illustrate, it also explains a large part of the controversy surrounding recent U.S. oil and gas policy.

In 1972 a coalition of New England governors joined the Consumers' Union in filing suit to abolish the United States' oil import control program. The publicly proclaimed goal of this federally enforced program (see chapter 7) was to obtain the lowest prices for crude oil and refined oil products consistent with a level of imports that did not endanger national security.[3] The New England governors and Consumers' Union contended that, in fact, its chief consequence had been to raise domestic oil prices and thereby force annual "transfers" (i.e., payments for which no productive services are rendered in exchange) of billions of dollars from citizens of oil-consuming states to citizens of oil-producing states. The fact that the governors of four of the largest oil-producing states—Louisiana, Oklahoma, Texas, and Wyoming—intervened on behalf of the defendant (i.e., in favor of federal enforcement of mandatory oil import controls), lends credence to the suspicion that at least some of their politically influential citizens were beneficiaries of a federally created privilege.[4]

The oil depletion allowance (see chapter 6) permits a standard deduction of 22 percent of the gross income (after deducting royalties) realized from the sale of all domestically produced crude oil and natural gas. According to a study recently completed for the U.S. Treasury, the net effect of this deduction has been to reduce the taxes paid by domestic oil and gas producers by about $1.4 billion per year.[5] By reducing taxes, the depletion allowance subsidizes the domestic production of oil and gas. The principal rationalization for this subsidy is that it encourages the development of additional domestic productive capacity, which can be used in the event supplies from foreign sources are interrupted by wars or other national emergencies. The Treasury-commissioned study, cited above, casts considerable doubt on the merits of this justification since it shows that the tax subsidy from oil and gas depletion allowances has resulted in annual additions to energy reserves worth only about $150 million.[6]

The two oil and gas policies just discussed do not exhaust the list of those giving rise to large income transfers. To illustrate, the Native Claims Act of 1971 promises to convey huge benefits to the relatively few Indians of Alaskan ancestry,[7] the Federal Power

Commission's price regulation of natural gas benefits those consumers fortunate enough to be able to obtain gas at its regulated below-opportunity-cost price, and the Jones Act taxes oil consumers in order to subsidize U.S. ship builders, owners, and crews. The next task of this chapter is to explain why huge income transfers are an inevitable consequence of most of the United States' present oil and gas policies.

RENTS AND RESOURCE COSTS

The sum of exploration, development, and operating costs measures the total resource costs that must be incurred when producing crude oil or natural gas. Exploration costs are incurred when productive factors such as labor and capital are used to search for new oil and gas reserves in areas where their presence is suspected but unsure. Development costs are incurred when facilities are constructed so that previously discovered reserves may be exploited. Operating costs are incurred when the previously developed production facilities are actually used to extract the oil or gas from its natural source. These resource costs are paid to the owners of the productive factors consumed in performing the three stages necessary for oil and gas production: exploration, development, and extraction. They are unavoidable if new energy reserves are to be found and produced.

In the United States, crude oil and natural gas are produced by many thousands of firms from a variety of heterogeneous geological sources. The fundamental technological constraint facing both industries is that there are sharp differences in the total resource cost (per Btu) of producing energy from these different sources. Large geological variations in the size and productivity (i.e., output per well) of American oil and gas fields are the chief causes of these cost differences. To illustrate, on the Alaskan North Slope exploration costs per barrel of newly discovered oil reserves promise to be low because there is a relatively high probability of giant (billion-barrel plus) oil fields being discovered. Moreover, because the Alaskan fields also appear capable of producing at high outputs per well—probably in excess of 10,000 barrels per day—the development and operating costs of producing each barrel ought to be low. These reasons explain why, in 1969, the President's Oil Import Task Force estimated that large quantities of Alaskan oil will have total resource costs of no more than 36 cents per barrel.[8] This is far less than the cost of producing oil from most other areas of the United States, where oil fields are smaller and usually far less productive. For example, many parts of Texas (onshore) are pocketed with small oil pools capable of producing only 5 to 10 barrels per well per day. Elsewhere I have estimated that the average resource cost of this oil was about $2.50 in 1969; it is even higher today.[9] In contrast, the average resource cost of each barrel of crude oil produced from the coastal waters of California, Louisiana, and Texas was only about $1.42.[10] Its lower costs stem from the fact that these offshore waters contain larger oil fields, and wells drilled into them are frequently capable of producing from 300 to 2000 or more barrels per day.

Every American crude oil or natural gas producer would like to produce exclusively from the very lowest cost sources. Nevertheless, most do not find it profitable to do so because the supply presently known to be available from such sources is far less than the current demand. This point is most easily shown by an example.

Suppose the oil industry is competitive and crude oil can be produced from only three fields: Field A can produce only 1000 barrels per day at a resource cost of 50 cents per barrel; field B can produce 1000 barrels per day at a resource cost of $1.00 per barrel, and field C can produce virtually unlimited quantities at a resource cost of $2.00 per barrel. If less than 1000 barrels are demanded (line D_1 in Fig. 4-1), firms will find it most profitable to produce oil exclusively from the lowest cost oil field; moreover, competition guarantees that consumers will pay only 50 cents per barrel for this oil. Suppose the economy grows, and next year 1500 barrels are demanded when the price is only 50 cents (line D_2). At this price, producers will be willing to produce a maximum of 1000 barrels because all barrels in excess of this amount cost at least $1.00 to produce. Thus, in order to persuade producers to expand output to more than 1000 barrels, consumers

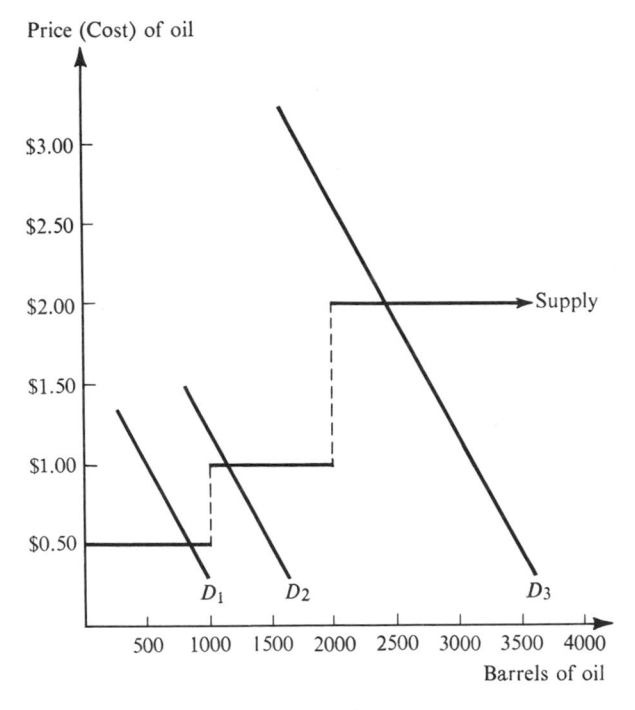

Figure 4-1. Rents and resource costs.

must be willing to bid up the price to at least $1.00. Finally, if demand rises even further (e.g., to D_3 in Fig. 4-1), oil's price will be bid up to $2.00 and firms will discover that it is profitable to begin producing from high-cost field C.

Suppose 2500 barrels of oil are demanded and sold when the price is $2.00. Then consumers pay $5000 for this oil. But what is the resource cost of producing it? The answer is the total sum that must be paid to productive factors for exploration, development, and extraction. In this example the resource costs of producing 2500 barrels would be $2500.[11]

Rents are defined as the difference between the total revenues earned from the sale of a product and the total resource costs incurred when producing it. Thus, rents refer to any surplus of revenues over and above the resource costs of producing any product. They arise whenever the supply of a product available from the very lowest cost sources is not sufficient to satisfy the demand. In such cases demand must be satisfied from higher cost sources and the owners of all cheaper sources will receive rents. Using the facts of our hypothetical example, total rents would be $2500 when 2500 barrels are sold at $2.00: Owners of field A—the most productive oil field—would receive $1500, and field B's owners would receive $1000, but field C's owners would receive nothing.[12]

The proclaimed goals of most of our oil and gas policies are to insure the availability of supplies adequate to satisfy future demand, to increase U.S.-produced supplies and thereby reduce the threat to our national security posed by possible import interruptions, and to prevent or reduce environmental pollution. Part II shows that many policies have sought to achieve these worthy goals either by taking steps that have indirectly raised the price of domestically produced oil or by giving subsidies to domestic oil and gas producers. Because of the fundamental technological fact of U.S. oil and gas supply—that even in the long run there are sharp differences in the total resource costs of the oil and gas produced from different sources—another consequence of these policies has been to raise the rents received by the domestic oil and gas interests by several billion dollars annually. In sum, enforcement of our current oil and gas policies has created and perpetuated very valuable privileges. What groups benefit from these privileges? What groups bear the costs?

INTEREST GROUPS

There are six identifiable interest groups whose economic well-being is directly affected by the fact that they either receive or pay for the privileges created by our oil and gas policies.[13] These groups are (1) owners of known or potential petroleum lands, (2) petroleum producers, (3) residents and taxpayers of the large oil and gas-producing states, (4) oil refiners and petrochemical producers, (5) suppliers of services (including labor) to the petroleum producers, and (6) petroleum consumers. Membership in all of these groups overlaps. Nevertheless, if asked to identify in which one of these six groups their predominant interests lie, most Americans would have a ready answer. Thus, this taxonomy should provide useful insights about the distributional consequences of U.S. oil and gas policies. Brief descriptions of the interests of each of these groups follow.

Owners of Oil Lands

In return for allowing the production of any petroleum products found on his land, the owner usually collects two kinds of rents: *Royalties* are charged which are a fixed percentage of the petroleum's wellhead price. Historically, depending on the region of the country, royalties have been set at either 12.5 percent or 16.66 percent of the wellhead price. *Lease bonuses* are bid by the producing companies in return for the privilege of being sole producer of any petroleum located on a specified land parcel. Whenever the level of the royalty is fixed by regional custom, the size of the lease bonus that the winning firm would bid will be a positive function of the expected present value of the rents to be earned from any petroleum produced from this land.[14] Other things being equal, the higher the probable selling price of the petroleum, and the lower its expected (private) costs of production, the higher will be the lease bonuses.[15] In sum, owners of oil and gas lands benefit from policies that are expected to raise prices because lease bonuses will be bid higher. If such policies prove successful, petroleum landowners enjoy a further increase in rents because royalties rise. Finally, they also benefit from policies that reduce the petroleum producers' costs, because these will persuade producers that it is profitable to offer a higher lease bonus bid.

The careful reader will note that I glossed over one important distinction between royalties and lease bonuses. It is that total royalties depend on the *actual* levels of prices and production, whereas total lease bonuses depend on the *expected* levels of prices and costs. That these expectations may not be realized has important distributional consequences for petroleum producers.

Petroleum Producers

The total rents earned from the sale of petroleum produced from a given land parcel depends on the quantity sold and the difference between its wellhead price and its resource costs.[16] Assuming competition among potential producers of petroleum and no uncertainty, the terms of the land-leasing contract would be worded so that all of the rents would be received by the landowner. Because of the low entry barriers, several thousand firms are in the business of producing oil and gas; hence, the assumption of competition seems reasonable.[17] However, at the time a contract is signed allowing an operating company to develop suspected petroleum lands, both future prices and production costs are uncertain. As a result, the terms of the land-leasing contract are designed to collect for the landowners all *expected* rents. In instances where the petroleum's wellhead price proves to be either higher than expected or its production costs lower than expected, some rents (i.e., higher profits) will also be collected by its producers.[18] Losses (i.e., lower profits) will be incurred by producers in the converse case.[19] Given these facts, the producers obviously have an interest in persuading governments to adopt or retain policies that raise crude oil's products' price (or prevent it from falling) above (below) its expected level. The same interest also leads producers to want governments to adopt and retain policies that lead to reduced production costs.

Residents and Taxpayers of Oil-Producing States

Four states—Texas, Louisiana, California, and Oklahoma—supplied nearly 80 percent of the total oil produced in the United States during 1972; Louisiana and Texas produced nearly 75 percent of our natural gas.[20] When the Alaskan pipeline is completed, Alaska will become our fifth large oil- (and eventually gas-) producing state. The "oil states" have two sources of large rents. First, on all state petroleum-bearing lands, which are extensive, they collect the landowner's rents already described. They also collect severance taxes on all petroleum produced within their borders.

When petroleum is taken (i.e., severed) from any land in a state, special severance taxes are imposed by the state in order to collect some of the oil land's rents. Severance taxes are in addition to the states' other corporation taxes. Like royalties, they are most frequently set at some percentage of the petroleum product's wellhead price. Thus, the state's severance tax collections will rise if this price goes higher. Revenues from severance taxes, royalties, and lease bonuses comprise a large fraction of the total revenues of the governments of the large oil- and gas-producing states.[21] Presumably, residents of these states are the beneficiaries.

Oil Refiners and Petrochemical Producers

The United States has restricted imports of crude oil. As a consequence, the right to import oil has been valuable (Chapter 7). The U.S. government gave most of these valuable oil import rights to oil refiners and petrochemical producers. Because the value of these rights was higher when the price of domestic oil was higher, the recipients of oil import rights had an interest in persuading governments to adopt policies that raised domestic oil prices. This served to offset (at least partially) their natural interest in having lower crude oil prices.

Suppliers of Services

The four groups already described share a common set of interests. Other things being equal, all benefit from policies that lead to higher petroleum prices; they also benefit from policies leading to lower production costs. The suppliers of services (including labor) to the petroleum-producing industry do not share both of these interests. They benefit from policies that cause a rise in the demand for their services. These are of two types: policies designed to stimulate petroleum demand and policies that raise the amount of services that must be consumed in order to produce any given output. Because this is a politically powerful interest group (especially in the legislatures of the "oil states"), the need to accommodate their different interests has influenced the form of several oil and gas policies.

Petroleum Consumers

Oil consumers pay the "rents" received by the five groups just discussed. Subsequent chapters show that their taxes are higher because oil and gas production is subsidized by an inefficient tax-break and that a variety of policies "work" by causing them to pay higher petroleum prices. In sum, these chapters will show that consumers are a large but powerless minority. Year in, year out, they have seen others benefiting from special treatment. Because consumers could do nothing to prevent this, their resentment has festered and grown.[22] It is difficult to exaggerate the importance of this accumulated and rankling resentment as a cause of the widespread discontent with our present oil and gas policies.

II

CURRENT U.S. OIL AND GAS POLICIES

5.

STATE AND FEDERAL LAND USE POLICIES

Two charges were repeatedly hurled in the round of accusations following the highly publicized oil spill off the Santa Barbara coast: the first was that the U.S. government was derelict in ever allowing oil drilling in the Santa Barbara straits; the second, a more restrained charge, claimed that the government was derelict in not requiring oil producers to satisfy far stricter oil-spill prevention standards. Since Santa Barbara, similar charges have been repeated in reference to federal or state support of such potentially important energy projects as offshore drilling in the Gulf of Mexico and the Atlantic coastal waters, commercial exploitation of the vast Western reserves of coal and oil shale; construction of a trans-Alaskan pipeline; and construction of new refineries, power plants, and "superports." The common element linking the debates over these and similar energy projects is that they can only be implemented by using "public" lands.

Narrowly defined, public lands are all lands owned by state or federal governments. Most of the United States' new reserves of crude oil and natural gas will be found on public lands located either in Alaska or in the coastal waters of the continental United States. Use of this land for the production and transmission of energy is costly because it requires us to forgo other possible uses.[1] Thus, the first question that should be addressed by our energy policymakers is which of these lands ought to be used to produce or transport energy? The government's (whether state or federal) pragmatic answer to this question has almost always been that public lands should be employed in their highest value uses. At first blush, this sounds like a decision-making criterion the citizenry should applaud. It is not; with the notable exception of some national park lands, the monetary worth of the public lands in their different possible commercial uses has usually provided the government's sole measure of value. Our government's facile acceptance of this valuation standard must be challenged because it provides a poor measure (or no measure) of such other valid public concerns as advancing national security, protecting our environment, and "improving" the income distribution. The need for challenging blind adherence to this "monetary worth" criterion is illustrated below, where the federal government's decision to authorize construction of a trans-Alaskan pipeline is critically evaluated. Also, there is an examination of the procedures actually used by governments to collect for their citizens any rents accruing from the commercial use of public lands.

Suppose the government has somehow decided what lands can be used for producing and transmitting energy. At this point a second land use question requires resolution: What specific restrictions should be placed on the commercial exploitation of public lands? Since energy projects frequently give rise to large external costs, the state has a legitimate interest in taking steps to insure that land use is appropriate, even if the project is undertaken exclusively on private lands.[2] Thus, when answering this question a broader definition of "public lands" seems appropriate. This definition includes all lands—publicly or privately owned—under the relevant governmental unit's political jurisdiction. The most important instance of such land use regulation—state market demand prorationing laws—is evaluated.

THE TRANS-ALASKAN PIPELINE

Background

In 1967 Atlantic Richfield and Exxon, U.S.A. discovered the Prudhoe Bay oil field on the Alaskan North Slope. Prudhoe Bay's

9.6 billion barrels of currently proved reserves are the largest known in North America. In contrast to the 30 barrels per day produced by the average U.S. well, each Prudhoe Bay well promises to yield roughly 10,000 barrels. Because of this high productivity, the resource costs of producing Prudhoe Bay crude will probably be less than 40 cents per barrel at the wellhead.[3] Since new oil presently sells in the U.S. for about $9.50 per barrel at the wellhead, enormous profits (rents) will be realized if this North Slope oil can be transported cheaply to U.S. markets. Because they realized that high profits were likely, in 1969 oil companies paid the state of Alaska an additional sum of more than $900 million for the right to produce any oil found on state lands in the Prudhoe Bay region.

The owners of oil land leases on or near the Prudhoe Bay field concluded that the cheapest way to deliver this oil would be to pipe it across the 900 miles of rugged terrain between the North Slope and Valdez (an ice-free port on the Alaskan Gulf). At Valdez it would be transferred to large tankers destined for the West Coast. The planned pipeline capacity was 2 million barrels a day, and the producers initially expected to start delivering this oil in 1972. These expectations were not realized because a coalition of environmental organizations obtained an injunction preventing the U.S. Interior Department from issuing the necessary construction permit until it had (1) evaluated the adverse environmental effects attributable to the pipeline and (2) examined the environmental impact of alternative means of supplying American consumers with similar quantities of energy. The Interior Department issued the necessary environmental impact statement in March 1972.[4] Having satisfied the formal requirements, it recommended that the trans-Alaskan pipeline should be built. The environmentalists appealed this ruling to the courts. In late 1973 Congress passed special legislation aimed at cutting short this seemingly interminable litigation. Oil should begin flowing through the trans-Alaskan pipeline in 1978.

The Alaskan North Slope is, at present, the most promising new domestic source of low-cost oil and gas supplies. In view of the severity of our current and projected domestic energy shortage, there can be no doubt that this valuable resource should be devel-

oped. Even the environmentalists who successfully delayed construction of the trans-Alaskan pipeline concede this point.[5] Between 1969 and 1973 the important policy question was what
would be the best way to deliver this oil to U.S. markets. The
choices were a 900-mile pipeline across Alaska and from there via
tanker to the U.S. West Coast or a 2500-mile pipeline across
Canada directly into the U.S. Midwest. The oil companies and the
U.S. and Alaskan governments favored the trans-Alaskan route;
environmentalists favored the trans-Canadian route. Which route
would have been in the best interests of the United States?

The Interior Department's environmental impact statement
upheld the environmentalists' contention that large oil spills would
be less likely if North Slope oil were shipped via a Canadian pipeline to the Midwest. Taken alone, this finding suggests that Interior Secretary Morton should have chosen to deny a permit for
construction of the Alaskan pipeline. But, he argued, overriding
economic and security considerations led him to do otherwise.

The Case for the Trans-Alaskan Pipeline

Advocates of the Alaskan pipeline advanced two economic
arguments for recommending its construction: (1) If an Alaskan
route was chosen, construction costs would total about $3.5 bil-
lion; choice of a trans-Canadian route would raise these costs to
about $6 billion. (2) Once construction was authorized, the Alas-
kan pipeline would take three years to complete; completion of the
lengthier Canadian pipeline would take four to six years. According to the Interior Department, each year's delay in delivering the
"low-cost" North Slope oil to the "lower 48" states would cost
Americans about $1.1 billion.[6] These two reasons were sufficient
to establish that the Alaskan pipeline would be much cheaper than
a much longer pipeline across Canada. But, as economist Charles
Cicchetti perceptively pointed out, this did not establish that the
Alaskan route was economically preferable—it ignored the fact
that Alaskan crude would command a much higher price in the
Midwest than on the West Coast.[7] On the basis of his detailed
studies, Cicchetti argued persuasively that the higher prices received for this oil in the Midwest would more than offset the

higher costs of transporting it there. Hence, contrary to Interior Secretary Morton's assertions, there was no overpowering economic argument favoring the Alaskan pipeline.

But what of national security? It now appears that the Alaskan pipeline will be in operation in 1977; had the Canadian route been chosen, it would not be ready until 1979 or 1980. Thus the U.S. would have been forced to import more OPEC oil during this two- to three-year period. Reliance on OPEC oil carries a much higher security risk.

The security argument in favor of the Alaskan route was advanced by General George Lincoln when he was director of the President's Office of Emergency Preparedness. "From a national security point of view," the general wrote Interior Secretary Morton, "it is important to get North Slope oil to our lower 48 states as soon as possible so as to lessen our dependence on potentially insecure foreign sources of petroleum." [8]

One consequence of the adoption of a Canadian route would have been greater dependence on imported oil between 1977 and 1980. What would have been the national security "cost" if the U.S. had not reduced its dependence on foreign oil during this period? The magnitude of this cost would depend upon the availability of alternative oil resources in the event of an import interruption.

Oil shipped via the Alaskan pipeline will be sold on the West Coast. In recent years, West Coast demand for oil has grown at an annual rate of 2.5 percent. (In contrast, demand for oil in the rest of the U.S. has grown at an annual rate of 5 percent.) Assuming that this rate of growth continues throughout the 1970s, West Coast crude oil demand would range from 2.5 million barrels a day in 1976 to 2.7 million barrels a day in 1980. If there were no shipments of North Slope oil between 1977 and 1980 because the government denied permission for construction of the Alaskan pipeline and no non-Canadian foreign oil was shipped to the U.S. because of some international crisis, there would still be at least four sources capable of supplying the West Coast with crude oil: The West Coast will be producing about 1,158,000 barrels per day; 400,000 barrels per day could be imported from Canada; at least 300,000 barrels per day could be supplied by withdrawing oil from the Naval Petroleum Reservation at Elk Hills, California; and at least 37,000 barrels per day could be imported from the adjacent oil-surplus Rocky Mountain states.[9]

The difference between total demand and the total supply from all available sources measures the oil deficit the West Coast would suffer in the unlikely event that all non-Canadian shipments of foreign oil were interrupted. Even if the Alaskan pipeline is not completed, this deficit is relatively small—ranging from only about 500,000 barrels per day in 1977 to 800,000 barrels per day in 1980.[10] Possible ways of meeting this deficit include storing additional emergency crude oil reserves, installing new production capacity for faster production of existing West Coast reserves including Elk Hills, and using rationing to force a small reduction in the West Coast's crude oil demand.

The above figures demonstrate that, even in the absence of any shipments of Alaskan North Slope oil, the West Coast would not be greatly endangered if non-Canadian foreign oil shipments ceased during any year between 1977 and 1980. This fact, coupled with the fact that a complete shutdown of foreign oil trade is probably unlikely, suggests that the early delivery of North Slope oil did not offer significant national security justification for favoring the Alaskan pipeline. When compared to the Alaskan pipeline, a Canadian pipeline offered tangible security and environmental benefits.

The Case for a Trans-Canadian Pipeline

In its study of the Alaskan pipeline, the Interior Department (citing OEP's General Lincoln) mentioned only two ways in which a trans-Canadian pipeline offered more security than the proposed pipeline across Alaska: First, pipeline shipments across Canada are less subject to interdiction by a hostile foreign power than are open-water shipments from Valdez.[11] Second, natural disasters (principally earthquakes) are less likely to interrupt the flow of North Slope oil if it is piped across Canada. This cursory analysis failed to recognize the most valuable security benefits of the Canadian route.

Three of the most likely sources of large quantities of additional secure oil for United States markets are the Alaskan North Slope, the Alaskan Gulf (in southern Alaska), and the Canadian Northwest (including the Arctic islands). The late Under Secretary of Interior William Pecora wrote that the crude oil potential of the Alaskan North Slope is 140 billion barrels and the potential of the Gulf of Alaska is 40 billion barrels.[12] Northwest Canada probably has potential reserves at least this large. Some idea of the magnitude of these estimated reserves can be inferred by comparing them with the 9.6 billion barrels of proved reserves at Prudhoe Bay.

The figures just cited make it obvious that coordinated development of these three major oil sources would help to meet future U.S. oil needs. There are two reasons why the choice of a Canadian pipeline for shipping Prudhoe Bay's oil would have promoted this goal, whereas the choice of an Alaskan route has worked against it:

1. The West Coast is the logical destination for both North Slope crude oil shipped via the Alaskan pipeline and for crude oil produced in the Alaskan Gulf. Transshipment of any of this oil from the West Coast to the rest of the U.S. would be extremely costly. In addition, even with no foreign oil imports, the West Coast will only demand slightly more than 1 million barrels a day of Alaskan oil in the late 1970s. These facts prompted the Interior Department to admit that substantial Gulf of Alaska production would cause "an inconvenient surplus [on the West Coast] if North Slope oil were to go there."[13] The implications of this are apparent: The expectation that the Alaskan pipeline would be constructed sharply reduced incentives for oil companies to press for exploration and development of new crude oil reserves in the Alaskan Gulf. On the other hand, a Canadian pipeline would deliver Prudhoe Bay oil to the Midwest rather than to the West Coast; in turn, this would spur development of Alaskan Gulf oil because this oil would be needed to meet the West Coast's demand.

2. The Interior Department's environmental impact statement estimated that if Prudhoe Bay oil were shipped via an Alaskan pipeline to the West Coast, daily imports of non-Canadian crude

oil into the rest of the U.S. would total about 8.5 million barrels in 1980. This region's dependence on "insecure" foreign oil would grow even larger in subsequent years. Currently the Alaskan North Slope and northwestern Canada are the two most likely sources for the additional large quantities of secure oil necessary to supply this oil-short region. United States energy policymakers should vigorously encourage production from both frontier sources. However, because a Canadian pipeline must first be built before oil from either of these sources can be shipped to the Midwest (and then to the rest of the U.S. east of the Rockies), and because the U.S. government has not promoted construction of this pipeline, current energy policy has actually had an adverse effect on the development of crude oil reserves in these frontier regions. This state of affairs would have been dramatically different if the U.S. had instead backed a Canadian alternative for delivering Prudhoe Bay oil. In sum, there were persuasive national security reasons for preferring a Canadian pipeline. Were there equally persuasive environmental reasons?

Oil shipped through the trans-Alaskan pipeline will traverse earthquake-prone regions and will have to be transhipped via tanker to the West Coast. The regions that would be traversed by a Canadian pipeline are not so seismically active as those in southern Alaska (near Valdez) and, if a Canadian route were chosen, transshipment via tanker would not be necessary. Hence, even supporters of the Alaskan pipeline confessed that a Canadian pipeline would be environmentally preferable because oil spills were less likely. However, they quickly rebuted this confession by arguing that mandatory safety measures would reduce these oil spill problems to minimum levels. Many of the technical submissions by critics of the Interior Department's environmental impact statement challenged the validity of this rebuttal.[14]

The highly vocal debate over the technical merits and demerits of the safety regulations required for the Alaskan pipeline clouded a much stronger environmental argument against the choice of an Alaskan route: Because of the large quantities of oil and gas known (or suspected) to be in northwestern Canada and the Alaskan North Slope, plans are already being developed to build both natural gas and crude oil pipelines across Canada to the U.S. It seems certain that one or both of these pipelines will be completed during the 1980s, whether the Alaskan pipeline is built or not. The damage to wildlife nesting patterns and migration flows, Arctic permafrost, and virgin wilderness could be cut roughly in half if all pipelines from the Arctic traversed a common corridor.[15] Since these other pipelines must go to the Midwest, these huge environmental savings would be possible only if the Alaskan pipeline were not built.

Conclusion

The case against the Alaskan pipeline was a strong one. The sole security benefit of the Alaskan route endorsed by the U.S. Interior Department was early delivery to the West Coast, which would not be suffering severe oil shortages in its absence. The Canadian line represented not only a more prudent approach to environmental problems but a long-term approach to meeting vital national energy needs.

The above discussion requires one qualification. A Canadian pipeline was possible only if the Canadian government approved. Because Canada probably has large oil and gas reserves in the northwest and because these can be sold (in large quantities) only if a pipeline is built linking this region with U.S. markets, Canada would appear to have an obvious interest in building such a pipeline. In view of our need for large quantities of both Alaskan and Canadian oil and gas, the United States government should have taken immediate steps to persuade Canada to permit construction of a Canadian pipeline. The big mistake of U.S. energy policy (with respect to encouraging the development of Alaskan North Slope oil) was its failure to take this step in 1969 or 1970. Because of the severity of U.S. oil security problems, if serious negotiations with Canada had not proved successful within one year of their initiation, the U.S. would have been negligent if it had not then taken all steps necessary to facilitate the speedy construction of a pipeline through Alaska. Alaskan oil was and is too valuable to allow interminable delays in its shipment.

COLLECTION OF RENTS ACCRUING TO
PUBLICLY OWNED MINERAL LANDS

After deciding which lands should be commercially developed, governments should have two further land-use goals: (1) insuring that production is economically and socially efficient and (2) collecting for their citizens any rents accruing to the publicly owned mineral lands. Failure to achieve this second goal gives rise to income transfers from the state to those few fortunate citizens "privileged" to develop publicly owned lands commercially. The public uproar throughout the 1920s over the Teapot Dome scandal illustrates the American citizenry's distaste for this kind of governmentally created privilege.[16]

In the United States, state and federal governments use a combination of royalties and lease bonuses to collect the rents on public lands where commercial quantities of petroleum are thought likely. For example, the U.S. government sets a fixed per-barrel royalty of at least 12.5 percent of the wellhead value of any petroleum produced from federal lands; it then awards exclusive rights to all oil on a given land parcel to the firm offering the largest lease bonus.[17] The major petroleum-producing states use nearly identical rent-collecting procedures. Huge rents are collected; to illustrate, two federal sales of petroleum land leases in the U.S. Gulf of Mexico netted the treasury about $2.25 billion during 1972.

Regardless of what rent-collecting procedure is utilized, if bidding is competitive and mineral rights are awarded to the highest bidder, there will be no income transfers from the state to the mineral land's private developers. Nevertheless, this fact does not imply that all rent-collecting procedures involving competitive bidding are equally desirable. Most desirable are those which encourage the private developer to produce the economically efficient level of output. Unfortunately, in the U.S., the universally used combination of competitive lease bonuses and a fixed percentage royalty causes output to be below the efficient level. Demonstration of this important result follows.

Economic efficiency requires that additional units of a product be produced as long as their cost is less than the product's price. In

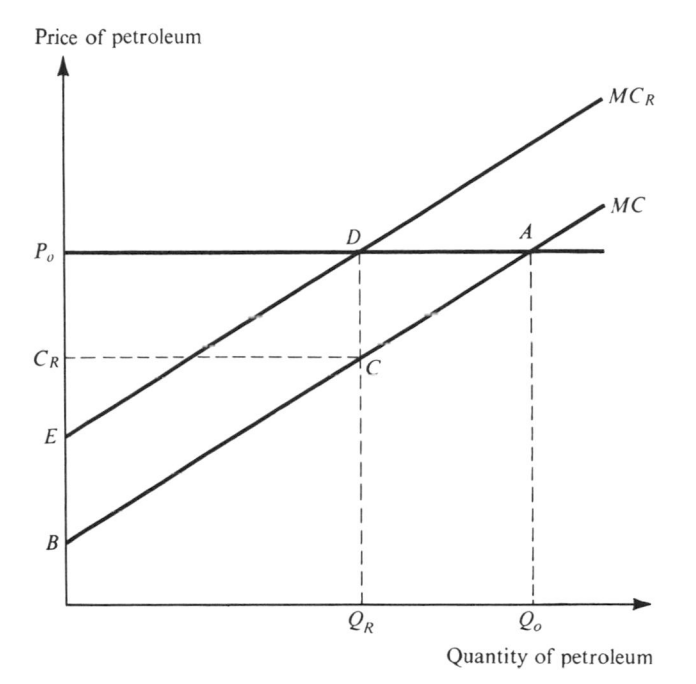

Figure 5-1. Petroleum land rents.

Figure 5-1, where the linear curve MC graphs the marginal cost of producing each unit of output from a hypothetical oil (or gas) field and P_o is assumed to be the market price for crude oil, Q_o is the efficient level of output.[18] If this output is produced, the maximum total rents would be equal to the area of triangle $P_o AB$. If the right to develop this land commercially were sold to the firm offering to pay the highest lease bonus, potential producers would find it profitable to bid up to $P_o AB$. Moreover, if these producers bid competitively, this would be the winning bid. Hence, the state would receive the maximum possible rent.

Suppose the state does not rely exclusively on competitive lease bonuses for collecting these rents. Instead, it follows present practice in the U.S. and uses some combination of a fixed percentage royalty and competitive lease bonuses. Then, the petroleum producer calculates the cost of each unit of output by summing (1) the marginal production cost of producing that unit and (2) the royalty payments he is charged when he sells that unit. MC_R graphs the producer's marginal cost curve. (It must lie above MC—the "real" marginal cost curve—whenever the royalty is positive.) Given these costs, the profit-maximizing producer desires to produce only Q_R units. Since the price received for the QRth unit (i.e., P_o) exceeds its real production costs (i.e., C_R), the decision to restrict output to this level is economically inefficient. The area of triangle DAC measures the lost rents because the use of both royalties and competitive lease bonuses causes the level of output to be inefficient.[19]

Any rent-collecting procedure that works, at least in part, by distorting producer's perceptions of the product's "true" marginal costs will cause them to produce an inefficient level of output; in turn, this leads to lower rents for the state. All feasible royalties or royalty-lease bonus combinations suffer from this defect.[20] But the exclusive reliance on competitive bidding for land leases does not. This raises a puzzling question: Why do American governments use an "inefficient" rent-collecting procedure?

Prior to large-scale commercial production, the rents that will actually be realized from the sale of all petroleum produced from any specified land parcel are uncertain. Promising sites sometimes yield dry holes; less promising ones sometimes become billion-barrel oil fields. In addition, even after the size and productivity of a given oil or gas field is known with reasonable certainty, its producers still face considerable uncertainty because changes in a variety of governmental policies (e.g., severance taxes, the depletion allowance, permissible wellhead prices for natural gas, import quotas, etc.) may lead to huge changes in profits. If the states and producers have different tastes toward risk or if their assessments of the magnitude of these risks differ, policies that permit shifting of some (or all) of the risk may be desirable. There is no obvious reason why producers should tend, on balance, to have stronger distastes for risk than do states. However, because the states (including the federal government) do control a variety of policies—which affect the profitability of any given petroleum investment—it does seem likely that their assessment of the magnitude of these risks would be less.

Petroleum producers may always avoid royalties by not producing. Therefore, if royalties are the state's sole method of collecting petroleum land rents, it bears all of the risk. Conversely, because lease bonuses are paid before any output is produced, if they are the state's sole method of collecting petroleum land rents, producers bear all of the risk. Obviously a combination of royalties and lease bonuses leads to a sharing of the risk. If, as seems likely, the state's assessment of the magnitude of all petroleum production risks is less than the potential producers', some combination of royalties and lease bonuses may be preferable to exclusive reliance on lease bonuses.[21] However, since any use of royalties always results in petroleum producers choosing an inefficient output level, an even more preferable rent-collecting procedure would be one that places the desired amount of risk on the state but does not cause producers to make inefficient output decisions. One such procedure, outlined below, is the two-part lease bonus.

Currently the entire lease bonus bid for any suspected petroleum property is paid prior to the drilling of any exploration wells. Because of the imprecise nature of the geological information available prior to drilling, uncertainty is usually high at the time of bidding. This uncertainty can be greatly increased because unforeseeable events may occur during the often lengthy time between payment of the lease bonus bid and the date when commercial production can begin. The time-lag problem is best illustrated by the huge interest costs and the high exploration and development expenditures borne by the oil companies who paid over $900 million for state oil land leases on the Alaskan North Slope in 1969; as of mid-1973 these companies still did not know when they would be able to produce commercially any oil that they have found or may find on these lands.

The state could transfer to itself any desired fraction of the risks just discussed by adopting a two-part lease bonus.[22] This bonus requires the state to sell petroleum land leases to the highest bidder (all royalties and severance taxes are abolished) but it would allow him to pay in two installments: Payment of the first installment would be demanded immediately, but payment of the second installment would only be required just prior to commencement of commercial production. At any time prior to this latter date, if the producer decides that commercial production would not be profitable at the lease terms he had previously agreed to, he would be allowed to cancel his outstanding lease bonus obligation merely by giving up any claim to the land. Of course, the state could then resell the petroleum rights to the highest bidder. Because it does not distort producers' perceptions of the oil's "true" marginal costs, the two-part lease bonus will not lead to an inefficient reduction in output. Moreover, since it does permit the state to shift any desired amount of risk from the producer to itself, the two-part lease bonus (or some more sophisticated variant) would be a better way for states to collect their petroleum land rents than the combination of royalties and competitive lease bonuses currently used.

STATE MARKET DEMAND PRORATIONING LAWS [23]

The common law of oil and gas ownership in the United States is premised upon the "rule of capture." That is, a landowner or his designee owns all the oil or gas he can pump out of pools located at least partially under his land. When the land overlaying a specified pool has many owners, each faces great financial incentives to produce the oil or gas as quickly as possible in order to prevent his neighbor from "capturing" it. As Adelman writes:

A well on one property would drain every adjoining lot; hence, you must drain your neighbor before he drains you. It is precisely like giving every retailer in a crowded commercial district the keys to every other retailer's stock. . . . Everybody must grab all he can and try to sell at any price in excess of bare operating cost. [24]

In absence of corrective laws or regulations, the "contradiction between many property holdings and the oil and gas which disregard them" always gives rise to two kinds of waste. First, production costs are higher because each producer has an incentive to overdrill his property in order to speed up his current rate of output and thus take away petroleum from his neighbor. In addition, besides wasting capital and labor, overdrilling leads to the physical waste of petroleum because the higher rate of current production is more than offset by lower rates of future production. This happens because overdrilling leads to the inefficient dissipation of the pressure necessary for driving petroleum from its natural reservoirs.

At least as early as 1916 it was recognized that enforcement of the rule of capture resulted in wasteful overdrilling whenever an oil field had more than one owner.[25] In order to eliminate this waste, large producers and landowners began a move to persuade the states to pass mandatory field unitization laws. Such laws require pooling of the ownership interests in each newly discovered reservoir before its commercial development is allowed. Then, the "unitized" reservoir is developed and operated by a single operator and all expenses and income are shared by the owners according to terms agreed upon in their unitization agreement.

Enforcement of mandatory field unitization laws would eliminate the wasteful overdrilling engendered by the rule of capture, because none of the landowners would be able to "capture" the reserves lying beneath the property of his neighbor. Nevertheless, such laws failed to pass during the 1920s, chiefly because of disputes among the property owners about what criteria should be used to determine ownership shares in unitized fields. This failure proved especially costly in the early 1930s as a result of the discovery and speedy development of the huge East Texas oil field. East Texas' ultimately recoverable crude oil reserves were in excess of 5 billion barrels. (Prior to the recent discovery of Alaska's Prudhoe Bay field, East Texas was the largest oil field ever discovered in North America.) Moreover, its ownership was widely dispersed. Because of the insidious effects of the rule of capture, each owner took steps to develop his property as quickly as possible. The result was a sudden large increase in supply. This, coupled with the fact that the onslaught of the Depression precipitated a sharp fall in crude oil demand, caused crude oil prices to plummet. Prices fell so low that some Texas and Oklahoma producers actually found it profitable to dump oil they could not sell into nearby creeks. Faced with this "conservation" crisis, the major oil-producing states of the U.S. Southwest (Texas, Louisiana, New Mexico, Oklahoma, and Kansas) abandoned their time-consuming and fruitless efforts to pass mandatory unitization laws and instead adopted a policy called market demand prorationing.[26] This policy was designed to give each state control over the total supply of oil produced by firms doing business within it. Market demand prorationing was initially justified as a conservation measure made necessary by the failure of private markets.

The mechanics of market demand prorationing are simple. First, the state uses a formula to establish each well's basic allowable daily production. The size of the "basic allowable" depends on two parameters: the well's depth and the number of acres it drains. Concern with cost differences rather than productivity differences provides the rationalization for the basic allowable formula: Because deep wells are more costly than shallow wells, and costs rise when more wells are drilled on a tract, the states felt that "fairness" required giving fields with deeper wells or more densely drilled tracts higher "basic allowables."

The states that established market demand prorationing did so to restrict the crude oil supply to the amount consumers were willing to purchase at a price each state deemed "just." This goal was not easily achieved because monthly crude oil demand fluctuated widely (owing to seasonal factors, etc.) and producers could always raise their basic allowables simply by drilling more and deeper wells. In addition, problems were likely to arise because oil produced in any specified state faced competition from oil produced in other states. Because of these complications, implementation of the basic allowable formula was not sufficient to give any state the desired control over price. Two additional tools were necessary.

The problem caused by fluctuating demands and changing supplies was solved by refusing to let each well produce its daily basic allowable. Instead, each month the major prorationing states ask the major purchasers of their crude oil how much they expect to buy in the following month. Using this information, the state estimates the statewide monthly market demand. It then calculates its monthly "market demand factor" by dividing its estimates of the total demand for its oil by the total of all basic allowables. Finally, each prorated well's actual output during the next month is restricted to the product of its basic allowable and the state's market demand factor.[27]

Use of the market demand factor gave each prorationing state a precision instrument for controlling the monthly output of its producers. Nevertheless, any given state's price-fixing policies were doomed to failure unless the major oil-producing states agreed to coordinate their respective prorationing practices. Failure to do so would have resulted in interstate competition for higher oil sales and, hence, lower prices. To forestall this possibility, the major prorationing states coordinated their activities through the offices of the Interstate Oil Compact Commission. They were assisted in these coordination efforts by the U.S. government.[28]

The oil states' enforcement of market demand prorationing did help to reduce the problems of overproduction that threatened the American oil industry during the 1930s. However, in the postwar period it became apparent that the remedy had proven far more costly than the illness it was designed to cure. The problems were of two kinds. First, prorationing did not eliminate the costly incentives for overdrilling. In fact, since oil fields with deeper and more closely spaced wells were rewarded with higher basic allowables and since inefficient stripper wells (i.e., wells producing less than 10 barrels per day) were exempted from all prorationing regulations, the incentives for overdrilling may actually have been strengthened.[29] Secondly, by using prorationing, the large oil-producing states were able to restrict severely their total output, and thereby succeeded in keeping prices for U.S. crude oil far above its competitive level throughout the late 1940s and early 1950s. Moreover, when rising imports threatened to destroy this state-enforced monopoly during the mid-1950s, the U.S. government again came to its rescue by imposing mandatory oil import quotas (chapter 7).[30] As a result, until the administration of the oil import quota program was effectively changed in 1971 and 1972, the prorationing policies of the major oil-producing states continued to play a key role in setting U.S. crude oil prices.

Enforcement of market demand prorationing continues to give rise to waste. However, it is far less of a problem today than it was just a few years ago.[31] In addition to the changes in oil import policy just alluded to, the other principal reasons for this problem's diminution are that the states' formulae for calculating "basic allowables" have been revised to reduce incentives for overdrilling and that because the U.S. demand for oil has recently grown much faster than domestic supplies, far fewer fields have had their output restricted below the levels their owners would desire.

SUMMARY

Federal and state governments must somehow resolve two fundamental land use questions: Which lands should be used for energy production, transmission, and consumption? What restrictions should be placed on their use? Because new variants of these two questions require almost daily answers, this chapter makes no attempt to provide a comprehensive critical evaluation of state and federal land use policies. Instead, the case studies herein critically analyze three of the most important land use policies actually promulgated in the United States. Besides their past and present importance, each of these policies was selected for study because it was adopted in order to resolve a serious land use problem, but in each case the policy actually chosen to alleviate these problems has proven a costly failure.

6.

TAX INCENTIVES

The American taxpayer has subsidized the oil and gas industry for more than 50 years. There are two major tax subsidies: percentage depletion and quick expensing of so-called intangible development costs. The proclaimed goal of both is to stimulate increases in domestic production and developed reserves. How well do they achieve this goal? [1]

TWO TAX SUBSIDIES

Percentage Depletion

The production of any scarce natural resource results in the depletion (i.e., using up) of a valuable asset. The depletion of their valuable oil and gas reserves is one of the costs borne by firms selling these products. It is a well-established tenet of American taxation that such costs are deductible from taxable revenues.[2] The resource owner profits from this deduction because it reduces his tax liability. The questions generating heated public policy debates are what should be the magnitude of these deductible costs?, how should they be deducted?

There are two basic types of depletion: cost and percentage. Cost depletion appeared as part of the first income tax in 1913 and has been available ever since as one method of calculating the deduction for recovery of capital. To calculate cost depletion it is first necessary to estimate the total quantity of the resource available. (This estimate may be revised later if it turns out to be wrong.) Then, each year the original invested capital is reduced by the ratio of the amount of the resource consumed that year to the total amount available. The capital reduction is deducted from income each year before determining the tax. Thus, at the same time the resource is completely consumed, the capital will be completely "written off" or "recovered" free of tax.[3] For most oil and gas investors there is a much better alternative: percentage depletion.

Percentage depletion is calculated by multiplying gross revenue from the sale of any natural resource by the applicable depletion allowance rate—22 percent for oil and gas.[4] The calculated depletion allowance bears no relation to the amount of the invested capital. On the contrary, it is completely open-ended. Thus, the producer of relatively productive petroleum properties frequently is able to deduct several times more than the value of his capital investment. The excess of the deduction allowed when the producer uses percentage depletion over the deduction allowed when he uses cost depletion times his marginal tax rate (for most firms almost 50 percent), is his tax saving or subsidy. This subsidy is estimated to have been $980 million in 1971.[5]

There are two limits to the operation of percentage depletion. The first is that the amount of the percentage depletion allowance cannot exceed 50 percent of the producer's taxable income calculated on the cost depletion basis. As illustrated by the examples below, this limit does not apply to the more productive and profitable low-cost wells. It only operates to cut off the subsidy for less profitable and marginal wells. The second limit was introduced by the Tax Reform Act of 1969 in the form of a minimum tax for tax preferences: The excess of the percentage depletion for any year over the written-down value of the capital (under the cost depletion method) is taxed at 10 percent, to the extent that such excess (including other items of preference as well) exceeds the sum of $30,000 plus total taxes.[6] Quantitatively, this limit has not proved very important.

Quick Expensing of Development Costs

Since 1918 the oil and gas industry has been given the option of deducting as current expense any "intangible drilling and development costs." [7] These include "wages, fuel, repairs, hauling, supplies, etc." associated with what is basically a capital investment—the drilling and preparation of wells for production.[8] (Also deductible are all costs associated with drilling "dry holes.") [9] Since most of these items would normally be capitalized and written off over the life of the successful wells, the option means that the producer may reduce his taxes in the current year rather than later. The net effect is to defer tax payments. The treasury estimated the tax deferment due to quick expensing at $340 million in 1971.[10] It is important to note the difference between tax deferments and subsidies. A tax deferment of $340 million means that the oil-and-gas industry gets to use that amount of money interest-free until the time when the tax authorities would "normally" allow it to be expensed. Its actual value to the recipient is the present value of the return it can earn when these deferred tax payments are invested. Since these taxes must eventually be paid, the annual subsidy attributable to quick expensing is considerably less than $340 million. (Its actual value depends on whether cost or percentage depletion is being used and on the productive life of the well.) On the other hand, the $980 million subsidy received through percentage depletion represents a permanent gain to the recipient, in most cases, petroleum landowners. Because of this large difference in importance, the rest of this chapter focuses primarily on the percentage depletion subsidy.

Example

An example should help to illustrate how the percentage depletion tax subsidy works. Suppose an oil company goes to three different locations and spends $200,000 in each location to bring in a well. Much of the $200,000 may be immediately expensed and any resulting loss on that well in the first year may be offset against the company's taxable profits on other ventures. If $80,000 remains as expenses for tangible items (e.g., drilling equipment,

Table 6-1 Tax Savings from Percentage Depletion: Three Examples

Well No. 1 (100 barrels/day)		Cost Depletion	Percentage Depletion
Revenues ($3.75/barrel)		$135,000	$135,000
Less: taxes and royalties	$25,000		
operating costs	90,000	115,000	115,000
Profit before tax and depletion		20,000	20,000
Less: depletion		4,000	8,000
Profit before tax		16,000	12,000
Tax		8,000	6,000

max 50%

Subsidy = $2,000, or 5.4¢/barrel

Well No. 2 (300 barrels/day)		Cost Depletion	Percentage Depletion
Revenues ($3.75/barrel)		$405,000	$405,000
Less: taxes & royalties	$ 75,000		
operating costs	194,000	269,000	269,000
Profit before tax and depletion		136,000	136,000
Less: depletion		4,000	66,000
Profit before tax		132,000	70,000
Tax		66,000	35,000

max 50%

Subsidy = $31,000, or 28.3¢/barrel

Well No. 3 (900 barrels/day)		Cost Depletion	Percentage Depletion
Revenues ($3.75/barrel)		$1,215,000	$1,215,000
Less: taxes & royalties	$225,000		
operating costs	419,000	644,000	644,000
Profit before tax and depletion		571,000	571,000
Less: depletion		4,000	267,000
Profit before tax		567,000	304,000
Tax		283,000	152,000

max 50%

Subsidy = $131,000, or 39.9¢/barrel

pipes, etc.), that must be capitalized and written off over time. Suppose that each well has a significantly different productivity. Table 6-1 shows that if the least productive well produces 100 barrels per day, the total revenues would be approximately $135,000 per year. Out of this amount, the operator must pay severance taxes and royalties of $25,000 and operating costs of $90,000. From the remaining $20,000 he deducts depletion in order to arrive at profit before tax. Assuming a life of 20 years and a steady annual production rate, cost depletion would be $4000 per year (i.e., one-twentieth of $80,000). This would leave $16,000 as profit before tax. Assuming that the producer's marginal profit tax rate is 50 percent, his annual tax liability would be $8000.

The maximum percentage depletion on a well grossing $135,000 would be $29,700 (i.e., 22 percent of $135,000).[11] If the well's owner were allowed to claim this deduction in full, he would pay zero taxes on the well's earning and would also enjoy a $9700 tax loss, which could be applied to reduce taxes owed on other income. But percentage depletion is limited to 50 percent of profit before tax when it is calculated using the cost depletion method. In the present example, profit before tax is $16,000. Thus, $8000 is the amount this well's owner can deduct. Because this deduction reduces his profit before tax to $12,000, his tax liability is $6000 instead of the $8000 under cost depletion. In sum, the privilege of using percentage depletion provides the owner with a subsidy of $2000 per year, or about 5.4 ¢ per barrel.

Suppose the second well is three times as productive as the first and total operating costs increase according to the "seven-tenths" rule.[12] Table 6-1 shows that percentage depletion gives an annual subsidy of $31,000, or 28.3 cents per barrel, to the owner of well number 2. Note that the rule limiting the amount of the percentage depletion deduction to 50 percent of taxable income calculated using cost depletion still limits the total deduction that can be claimed. However, the relative cost to the well's owners of this rule is not nearly so high when he owns the more productive well number 2. Specifically, the full depletion allowance would have provided a deduction of $89,000 (i.e., 22 percent of $405,000), or only about one-third more than the amount allowed under the 50 percent of taxable income limit.

Finally, suppose the third well is three times as productive as the second (i.e., nine times as productive as the first) and total operating costs continue to increase according to the "seven-tenths" rule. Table 6-1 shows that percentage depletion gives an annual subsidy of $131,000, or 39.9 ¢ per barrel. Note that for this

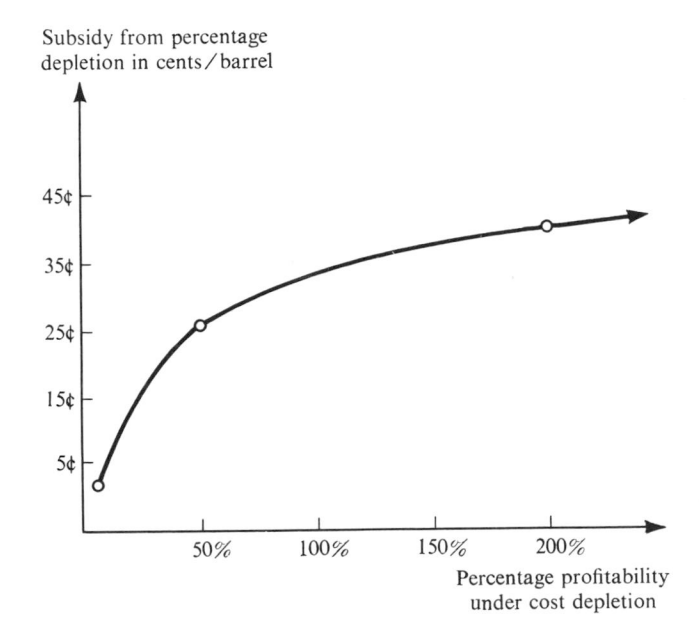

Figure 6-1. Relationship between a well's profitability and the subsidy it receives from percentage depletion.

very profitable well the company may deduct the full percentage depletion allowance (i.e., 22 percent of $1,215,000) since this amount does not exceed the 50 percent limit.

An approximate measure of each well's profitability if it were not allowed to claim percentage depletion may be computed by dividing profit after tax using cost depletion by the original outlay of $140,000 (i.e., $200,000 less the $60,000 tax saving from expensing $120,000 of intangibles). The profitability for the three wells, if they were given no percentage depletion tax subsidy, would be approximately 6, 47, and 202 percent respectively. Figure 6-1 plots the approximate shape of the percentage depletion tax subsidy as a function of each well's profitability. It is higher for more profitable wells. Suppose we decide that oil-and-gas production should be subsidized; would we want a subsidy like this? I will return to this question after discussing briefly the historical background of percentage depletion.

BACKGROUND

How did we come up with this system? Professor Charles Galvin provides a succinct summary of the early history:

The percentage-depletion concept evolved from the concept of discovery depletion introduced in the Revenue Act of 1919. Taxpayers were permitted the deduction for depletion based not on investment but upon the value of the property thirty days after discovery of new deposits. The measure was responsive to requests for benefits for exploration and discovery of minerals during World War I; it was, therefore, not an accounting device for cost recoupment but an incentive device built into the federal revenue system to permit tax-free receipts in excess of cost as a bonus for discovery. In interpreting the law considerable administrative leniency was exercised in regard to what was "discovery" and what was "value." New wells in old fields that defined more precisely the boundaries of the reservoir were categorized as discovery wells. Value was geared to oil prices inflated by World War I, so that the tendency was to overvalue properties on the long-run basis and permit a disproportionately high depletion deduction in relation to postwar revenue from the properties. The result was that taxpayers in the post-World War I years were using depletion deductions against other income. The congressional response to this situation in the Revenue Act of 1921 was to limit the annual deduction to the amount of the net income from the particular depletable property. By the time of the 1924 Act the national prosperity and economic expansion made the incentives of war less significant. The Treasury reported that mineral taxpayers were using the depletion deduction to pay little or no tax on mineral extraction, and Congress reduced the maximum deduction allowable to the present fifty percent of net income.

By 1925 there developed a general disenchantment with the discovery-value method. The report of the investigation of the Bureau of Internal Revenue in that year stated that administrative discretion had been exercised without regard for standards or precedent and that too many decisions turned on individual judgment with correspondingly erratic results. Some substitution was necessary. To the extent that there had been any formularization of the discovery-value method, it had usually been based on discounting expected future income. This technique was translated into an annual discount through the percentage-depletion formula with the carry-over of the 50 percent net-income limitation from the 1924 Act.

There was some suggestion that the 27.5 percent compromise between the advocates of 25 percent and those of 30 percent just about corresponded to the mean percentage experience under the discovery-value method. There were, however, data that discovery allowances varied widely, having run as high as 60 percent of gross income. In retrospect it seems fair to say that the choice of 27.5 percent was largely fortuitous. [Footnotes omitted.] [13]

After many unsuccessful attempts to reduce or eliminate percentage depletion, the Tax Reform Act of 1969 reduced the rate from 27.5 percent to 22 percent. In proposing that the rate be reduced to 20 percent, the House of Representatives stated the general reasons for the change:

Your committee believes that even if percentage depletion rates are viewed as a needed stimulant at the present time they are higher than is needed to achieve the desired beneficial effect on reserves. In recent years the petroleum industry, which reports on corporate tax returns, has paid taxes to the United States and foreign governments amounting to about 21 percent of taxable net income. This compares with an average tax of over 43 percent paid by manufacturing companies not eligible for various kinds of special tax treatment. Although there are other reasons for this difference in taxes, percentage depletion is the most important single reason for the lower rates paid by the petroleum industry.

Your committee believes that there is need to strike a better balance than now exists between the objective of encouraging the discovery of new reserves and the level and revenue cost of percentage depletion allowances. The present 27.5 percent percentage depletion rate for oil and gas wells was set up in 1926 when tax rates were substantially lower than at present. As a result, the tax inducement granted by this percentage depletion is substantially greater now than it was in 1926. . . . These new percentage depletion rates will still provide substantial encouragement for the exploration and discovery of new reserves of oil and gas and the minerals concerned. Moreover, these new rates will be more realistic in relation to the need for such encouragement. Stated another way, the reduction in percentage depletion rates provided by your committee's bill should have only a minimal effect on efforts to discover new reserves. [14]

The Senate thought 23 percent would be more appropriate. [15] The two versions went to the conference committee, which again compromised by splitting the difference. [16] The revenue loss for 1970 from percentage depletion was estimated by the Treasury at $1.47 billion.[17] The reduction to $980 million in 1971 reflects the impact of the 1969 Act.[18]

The 1969 Tax Reform Act also eliminated two other tax subsidies given to petroleum producers: special treatment of "production payments" and the so-called "ABC transaction." [19] The resulting increase in tax revenues was estimated at $100 million in 1970.[20] No change was made in the option to deduct intangible drilling expenses. The House had proposed eliminating the percentage depletion allowance for oil and gas deposits located outside the United States.[21] This was rejected by the Senate after it noted that all the benefit would go to foreign governments:

The committee . . . does not believe it is desirable to eliminate, as the House bill would do, percentage depletion on foreign oil and gas wells. This probably would not result in a significant increase in U.S. revenues, since foreign countries probably would raise their tax rate on income from oil and gas production and thereby reduce, because of the foreign tax credit, any additional revenues the United States might receive. Indeed, the committee was advised that some countries have provisions in their taxing programs automatically increasing their tax to take advantage of higher U.S. taxes which can be offset by our foreign tax credit. Thus, the end result of eliminating percentage depletion on foreign oil and gas deposits would merely be to increase the foreign tax burden imposed on U.S. businesses. This result is indicated by the fact that while the U.S. revenue gain from this provision of the House bill is expected to be $25 million in 1970, it is expected that by 1972 this U.S. revenue gain will have decreased to a negligible amount.[22]

EFFICIENCY OF PERCENTAGE DEPLETION AND QUICK EXPENSING

The principal justification for percentage depletion must be that the increases in petroleum production and the reserves it stimulates are large enough to justify its $980 million annual cost. When evaluating this justification's plausibility, it is important to keep in mind the basic principle that the most important economic decisions are those made at the margin. If we want someone to look for a new oil field, then we want him to look where he otherwise

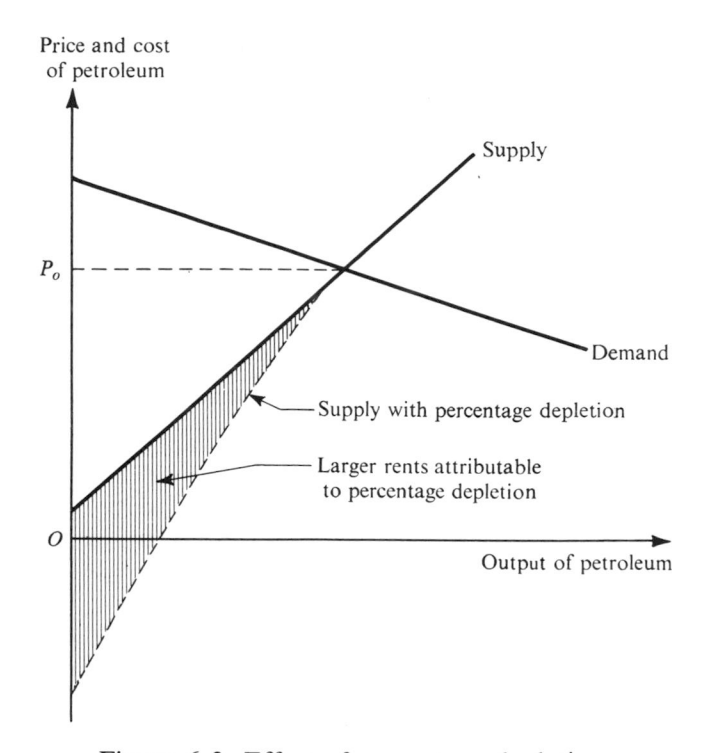

Figure 6-2. Effect of percentage depletion.

would not. Similarly, if we want to keep more wells operating, we are interested in persuading those who own marginal high-cost wells to continue operating them. And, if we want to affect prices, we are interested in reducing the costs of the marginal producers who determine the price. In sum, if we have $980 million to spend for stimulating oil and gas supplies, then we wish to spend it where it will have the most effect—at the margin.

The key flaw with percentage depletion is that it is not directed at influencing marginal decisions. Rather, as the derivation of Figure 6-1 illustrates, it gives the greatest rewards to the lowest-cost, highest-profit producers. Giving a much lower per-barrel subsidy to the high-cost marginal producers sharply reduces the probability that much of the percentage depletion subsidy will be competed away.[23] Moreover, since the oil that is expected to be low cost (i.e., any oil expected to cost appreciably less than its anticipated selling price) will be produced whether or not it is subsidized, it seems unlikely that percentage depletion will lead to an appreciable increase in petroleum reserves or output.

Looking at the evidence just summarized, a skeptic might conclude that percentage depletion is really intended to raise the petroleum landowners' rents and not to raise domestic output or lower prices (Figure 6-2).[24] This conclusion is reinforced by the results of a major study commissioned by the U.S. Treasury from the CONSAD Research Corporation. CONSAD concluded that at a time when percentage depletion provided oil and gas producers with an annual subsidy of more than $1 billion, it resulted in annual additions to energy reserves that were worth only about $150 million.[25]

In contrast to its very negative assessment of the efficiency of percentage depletion, CONSAD concluded that quick expensing of intangible development costs was a rather efficient tool for stimulating petroleum output. Because marginal wells, on balance, require heavier capital investments to produce a given quantity of petroleum, the privilege of quick expensing gives them a larger per-barrel subsidy. Thus, CONSAD's findings are not surprising.

CONCLUSION

Percentage depletion is the principal tax subsidy granted to the U.S. petroleum industry. Because it rewards only a small minority of our citizens—chiefly petroleum landowners—and does not lead to an appreciable rise in output or reserves, it should be abolished. On the other hand, quick expensing of development costs appears to be a relatively efficient way of subsidizing higher domestic petroleum output. If this were a desirable goal, this tax subsidy should be continued. However, since a major cause of our "energy crisis" stems from the fact that our current and projected high rates of energy consumption have as unfortunate by-products both increased levels of pollution and increased reliance on insecure foreign oil and gas, Part III will argue that even "efficient" petroleum tax subsidies are undesirable.

7.

OIL IMPORT
POLICY

BACKGROUND

Crude oil prices plummeted in the early 1930s. The Depression led to a sharp fall in demand, and this fall coincided with a sharp increase in supply, brought on largely by development of the huge East Texas oil field. As chapter 5 noted, the major oil-producing states passed market demand prorationing laws to alleviate the resultant economic distress. These "conservation" measures established state commissions, which in turn passed regulations restricting, often severely, maximum rates of production from each well. As long as the leading oil-producing states were able to coordinate their respective prorationing policies, high crude oil prices could be successfully maintained. Since the supply curve of U.S.-produced oil was relatively price-inelastic (see chapter 4), this meant that large rents were received by many of the domestic oil interests.[1] In the future, they would take steps to prevent their erosion.

Prior to the late 1940s the United States was self-sufficient in crude oil; the Gulf Coast states actually exported large quantities to Western Europe. But, during the late 1940s their share of the Western European market was quickly eroded by expanding imports from lower-cost Persian Gulf sources. By 1950 Persian Gulf oil was supplying most of Western Europe's petroleum needs. Having won nearly total control of the Western European market, some Persian Gulf producers began exporting to the U.S. The result was rising American oil imports, which had the effect of undermining the oil states' previously successful efforts to fix a high price for U.S. crude.[2] Specifically, in the face of swelling imports, American crude oil's high price could be maintained only by continually tightening the state's prorationing policies. But, even if they succeeded in doing this, the domestic industry knew its profits would fall with a fall in domestic oil's market share. Thus, the domestic "oil interests" sought to end the erosion of their product's market share by persuading the U.S. government to drastically restrict oil imports. Obviously, it would not be politic to confess that their motives were anything but idealistic. Hence, starting in the early 1950s, they advanced the argument that the U.S. must be protected from higher oil imports because rising dependence on "insecure" foreign oil threatened national security. Chapter 2 has already explained why the national security rationale for oil and gas policies had almost no validity prior to the mid-1960s. Indeed, even as late as 1969 most students of this industry agreed with Milton Friedman's conclusion that "the political power of the oil industry, not national security, is the reason for the present subsidies to the industry. International disturbances simply offer a convenient excuse." [3] Nevertheless, accepting the then spurious national security rationale *in toto,* a Cabinet advisory committee recommended the use of voluntary oil import quotas in 1955.

Imported oil was far cheaper than domestic; hence, high profits awaited any who violated the voluntary quotas. Because the voluntary quotas had no effective sanctions, this incentive to "cheat" soon proved strong enough to cause them to fail. Facing overwhelming political pressure from the domestic beneficiaries of high crude oil prices whose interests were thereby threatened, President Eisenhower responded by establishing a mandatory oil import control program in 1959.[4] In a release accompanying his proclamation the President stated:

> The new program is designed to insure a stable, healthy petroleum industry in the United States capable of exploring for and developing new hemisphere reserves to replace those being depleted. The basis of the vol-

untary program, is the certified requirements of our national security which make it necessary that we preserve to the greatest extent possible a vigorous healthy petroleum industry in the United States.[5]

In a decision that was to have major political ramifications in the future, President Eisenhower decided that the rights to import the limited amount of foreign oil permitted under the quotas should be allocated by giving them to refiners, and later, to petrochemical producers.[6]

Because of its distance from the petroleum sources near the Gulf Coast, residents of New England have always paid relatively more for refined oil products and natural gas than residents of other parts of the U.S. Also, not owning any oil lands, they do not receive any of the oil rents. As a result, the New England congressional delegation has consistently spearheaded the attack against oil import quotas. In 1968 Occidental Petroleum proposed a plan that it claimed would reduce New England's heating oil prices 10 percent: Occidental would build a 300,000 barrels per day refinery at Machiasport, Maine, if it were granted rights to import 100,000 barrels of crude oil each day.[7] Under the 1969 quota allocation formula, Occidental's proposed Machiasport refinery would have been allowed to import less than 30,000 barrels of oil daily. Since the right to import one barrel of oil was worth about $1.50 in 1969, acceptance of Occidental's request would have rewarded it with an additional daily subsidy in excess of $100,000. Since total oil imports were strictly limited by the quota, Occidental could have been rewarded more import rights only if other refiners were rewarded less. Thus, the entire additional subsidy requested by Occidental would have been at the expense of subsidies already being received by other refiners.

After announcement of Occidental's Machiasport plans the battle proceeded; New England supported Occidental's proposal, and the oil states and oil refiners strongly opposed it. In an effort to resolve this ticklish battle over the distribution of the fruits of a federally created "privilege," President Nixon established a prestigious Cabinet task force to undertake the first comprehensive review of U.S. oil import restrictions.[8] Before examining the Oil Import Task Force's policy recommendations and the subsequent actions of the President, it is useful to analyze the costs of oil import quotas in more detail.

COST OF OIL IMPORT QUOTAS

Enforcement of import quotas encouraged domestic crude oil producers to produce higher outputs by restricting the price competition offered by foreign oil. More precisely, by restricting imports, the demand for domestic crude oil was effectively raised and this higher demand could be satisfied only by a rise in domestic output. The enhancement of national security attributable to this higher domestic output was the alleged benefit from an import control policy. Its cost was higher petroleum prices because domestic producers would have found it profitable to raise output only at a higher price.

The long and acrimonious debate over the wisdom of the United States' policy of enforcing mandatory oil import controls was punctuated by widely differing, often partisan, estimates of this program's cost. In principle, it ought to have been an easy task to compute the cost of oil import quotas to American consumers at any given time. To do so, one needed only to calculate the difference between the total cost of crude oil sold in the United States under the import control policy and the total cost if this policy were abolished.[9] The total cost of crude oil sold in the United States at any specified time is equal to the product of the number of barrels sold in the United States multiplied by its average price per barrel. This cost may be estimated with a high degree of accuracy. Therefore, the principal cause of the widely differing estimates of the costs of oil import quotas must have stemmed from different estimates about what would be the price of crude oil in the absence of quotas.

President Nixon's Oil Import Task Force estimated that the United States' mandatory oil import controls cost U.S. consumers roughly $4.8 billion in 1969.[10] This estimate was arrived at by adding the products of estimates of what would have been the total per barrel reduction in each region's crude oil costs if all oil import controls were eliminated and that region's crude oil consumption.

The Oil Import Task Force used a two-step argument to estimate what would have been the per barrel reduction in each region's crude oil costs if import controls were abolished. First, it observed that during 1969 the actual differences between the delivered cost to refiners of equal quality barrels of domestic and foreign crude oil were approximately $1.50 in District I, $1.05 in Districts II–IV, and $0.85 in District V.[11] Second, it inferred that if unlimited quantities of foreign oil were available in each of these regions at these lower prices, then competition would have forced corresponding reductions in the price of domestic oil.

Both critics and advocates of the policy of mandatory oil import controls agreed that the Oil Import Task Force used the correct methodology when estimating this policy's total consumer costs. Therefore, any disagreement with its cost estimate must stem from disagreement with the Task Force's explicit assumption that if import controls were abolished, the delivered price of foreign crude oil would be the same as it was actually observed to have been with the present quotas. Spokesmen for the American oil industry and for several of the largest oil-producing states challenged this assumption. They asserted that if import controls were abolished and the United States became appreciably more dependent upon foreign oil supplies, the major oil-exporting nations would charge a sharply higher price. Hence, they concluded, the Oil Import Task Force overestimated the import control's "true" cost.

The Task Force critics' argument was premised on the assumption that broadening the market for foreign oil by increasing the number of buyers would lead to increased monopoly power and therefore higher prices. The critics' argument was weakened because a contrary one was equally plausible. That is, because American oil import quotas restricted the size of the potential market available to oil from foreign countries, collusion was encouraged in order to prevent competition that would lead to lower prices but unchanged imports.[12] Acceptance of this argument implies that if U.S. oil import controls were abolished, each oil-exporting country would have been more apt to believe that it could earn higher profits by reducing its prices slightly and thereby garnering sharply higher U.S. sales. This belief ought to have made collusion much more difficult. As a result, the delivered price of foreign oil would fall and thus the total savings reaped by American consumers would exceed the Task Force's $4.8 billion estimate.

The above discussion points to a seemingly unavoidable dilemma facing all who attempted to evaluate the United States' oil import policy: Whose consumer cost estimates should be believed? However, as the following example will show, one did not need to answer this very difficult question in order to conclude that mandatory oil import quotas were an especially bad device for achieving any desired increase in U.S. oil output.

The United States produced about 4 billion barrels of crude oil (including natural gas liquids) in 1972. This oil sold at an average price of about $3.75 at the wellhead. Assuming no other policies were changed, what would have been the extra cost to American consumers if oil import quotas were tightened sufficiently to persuade U.S. producers to raise their output by 10 percent, to 4.4 billion barrels? What would have been the net savings enjoyed by consumers if the import quotas were instead relaxed so that U.S. producers would choose to reduce their output by 10 percent, to 3.6 billion barrels? In order to answer such questions it is necessary to know the shape and position of the long-run supply curve of U.S.-produced crude oil. For purposes of illustration, assume that this curve is as illustrated in Figure 7-1. Then, the area of rectangle $P_A Z W P_B$ measures the additional consumer costs because tighter import quotas are enforced in order to obtain an additional 400 million barrels of domestic crude oil output.[13] It should be stressed that these costs are in addition to those paid by consumers when these 400 million barrels were imported rather than produced domestically. That is, they are extra costs that must be paid even though the total amount of oil (domestic production plus imports) available for U.S. consumption remained unchanged. The largest part of these additional costs, trapezoid $P_A Z Y P_B$, represents transfer payments to domestic oil interests. These transfers arise because oil import quotas work by raising the price of crude oil consumed in the U.S. and thus they also raise the rents received on all barrels that would have been supplied at a lower price. The area

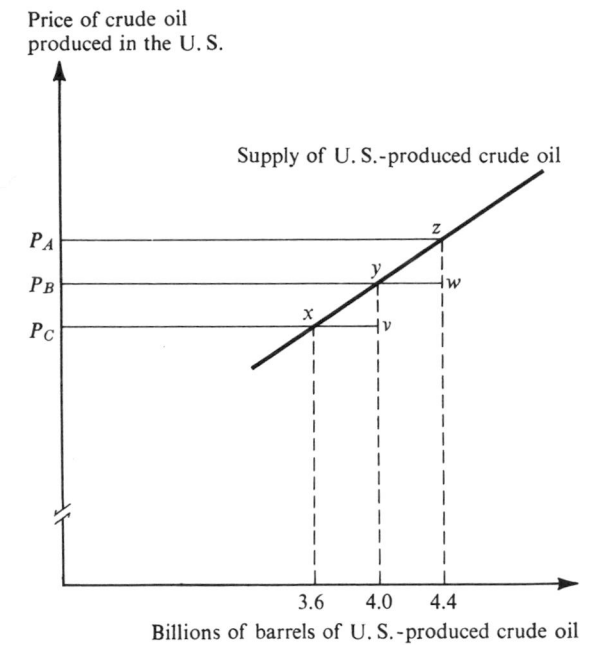

Figure 7-1. Cost effects of two incremental
changes in the level of U.S. oil imports.

of triangle *YZW* measures the additional payments necessitated by
the higher resource costs of expanding domestic output.[14] An explanation similar to the one just offered leads to the conclusion that
the area of rectangle $P_B YVP_C$ measures the consumer cost savings
because oil import quotas are relaxed; the area of trapezoid
$P_B YXP_C$ measures the component of these savings attributable to
lower transfer payments.

Tables 7-1 and 7-2 show, respectively, how the magnitude of
the consumers' costs or savings depends crucially on the price-
elasticity of the U.S.-produced crude oil supply. The results of
several empirical studies suggest that in the range of current output
the price-elasticity of the United States' crude oil supply is near
zero in the short run (a one- to two-year period); even in the long
run it is thought to be a bit less than one.[15] If these results are
roughly correct, Tables 7-1 and 7-2 confirm that oil import quotas

Table 7-1 Added Annual Cost to American
Consumers of a 400-Million-Barrel Reduction
in the Annual Level of U.S. Oil Imports

| | Price-Elasticity of U.S. Crude Oil Supply | | |
	0.5	1.0	5.0
Added resource costs	$150 million	$75 million	$15 million
Added transfer payments	$3.15 billion	$1.575 billion	$315 million
Total added consumer costs	$3.30 billion	$1.65 billion	$330 million

Table 7-2 Annual Savings Enjoyed by American
Consumers Because of a 400-Million-Barrel
Increase in the Annual Level of
U.S. Oil Imports

| | Price-Elasticity of U.S. Crude Oil Supply | | |
	0.5	1.0	5.0
Resource savings	$150 million	$75 million	$15 million
Transfer savings	$2.85 billion	$1.425 billion	$285 million
Total consumer savings	$3.0 billion	$1.50 billion	$300 million

were very costly to American consumers—primarily by causing
huge income transfers, which the government confessed (chapter
4) were undesirable in the absence of clear public policy justification.

In addition to the large income transfers just discussed, the giving away of scarce oil import rights also transferred income to
their fortunate recipients—chiefly domestic oil refiners and pe-
trochemcial producers. These transfers arose because the recipients
could sell imported oil at a price greater than its cost. Because of
this price-cost differential, the right to import one barrel of crude
oil sold for about $1.50 in 1969. Since crude oil imports were
nearly 400 million barrels, the Oil Import Task Force estimated

that transfers to refiners and petrochemical producers totalled almost $600 million in 1969.[16]

Arguments over the proper division of the high-income transfers resulting from enforcement of oil import quotas were inevitable. They were of two types. On the one hand, those living in regions of the U.S. that produced little or no oil complained that the prices they paid for refined oil products were unfairly high; the "oil interests" strongly disagreed. On the other hand, each of the different types of recipients of the valuable oil import rights repeatedly offered reasons why its type was deserving of a higher share. These two arguments merged after the Machiasport controversy.

THE FAILURE OF U.S. OIL IMPORT
POLICY: 1970–1973

After concluding its study of the United States' oil import policy in Spring 1970, President Nixon's Oil Import Task Force recommended that oil import quotas should be phased out quickly and replaced with a high but declining tariff. After studying this recommendation for several months, the President rejected it.[17] In light of this decision it is rewarding to reread the Oil Import Task Force's damning indictment of the United States' oil import policy.

The present import control program is not adequately responsive to present and future security considerations. The fixed quota limitations that have been in effect for the past ten years, and the system of implementation that has grown up around them, bears no reasonable relation to current requirements for protection either of the national economy or of essential oil consumption. The level of restriction is arbitrary and the treatment of secure foreign sources internally inconsistent. The present system has spawned a host of special arrangements and exceptions for purposes essentially unrelated to the national security, has imposed high costs and inefficiencies on consumers and the economy, and has led to undue government intervention in the market and consequent competitive distortions. . . . If import controls are to serve the distinctive needs of national security, they should be subject to a system of federal control that interferes as little as possible with the operation of competitive market forces while remaining subject to adjustment as needed to respond to changes in the over-all security environment. A majority of the Task Force finds that the present import control system, as it has developed in practice, is no longer acceptable. The basic question, then, concerns the character and degree of import restriction judged necessary to safeguard the nation against severe economic weakening or supply deprivations.[18]

Events that transpired between 1970 and 1973 further validated these criticisms. Ultimately, as the next section shows, they led the President to adopt a new oil import policy.

The United States' crude oil demand has grown rapidly since President Nixon decided to retain oil import quotas; over the same period there has been no appreciable increase in U.S.-produced supplies. The result, if President Nixon had, in fact, kept the 1969 formula for calculating the permissible level of oil imports unchanged, would have been either sharply higher oil prices or rationing. Since both alternatives were judged unpalatable, the President modified the overall oil import formula by periodically liberalizing the quota so that imports could fill the gap between domestic supplies and market demand at a politically acceptable price. As a result of this decision, oil imports rose at an average annual rate of nearly 20 percent from 1970 to 1973. Much of this increased supply came from "insecure" OPEC countries. Because OPEC has become a strong cartel, sharply rising imports now pose two different types of threats to the United States' oil security. First, if there are any import interruptions, economic havoc promises to become much more severe because import dependence has risen. Secondly, the United States has become more dependent on imported oil, thus reducing its bargaining power with OPEC and increasing the probability that either an economically or politically motivated boycott will occur.

This erosion of bargaining power is best illustrated by the events surrounding the Teheran-Tripoli agreements reached in early 1971. The international oil companies had entered these negotiations in order to persuade the OPEC countries not to carry out their threat to cut off all oil supplies. The negotiations were concluded by an agreement in which these companies agreed to pay an additional 50 cents per barrel in return for a guarantee that over the next five years there would be only moderately rising prices. Chapter 2 has discussed how the promised five-year peace lasted only a few months.

In addition to allowing, largely by default, growing reliance on oil imports from insecure sources, the President's administration of the oil import program reduced the United States' oil security in at least three other ways.

First the import control program allowed (indeed encouraged) enormous differences in the import dependence of different sections of the country. In particular, the East Coast has become very dependent on oil imports. If imports continue to grow at recent rates, the East Coast's oil demand will soon be satisfied almost entirely from insecure non-Canadian foreign sources.[19] In stark contrast, the Gulf Coast states and their neighbors will be consuming only domestic oil. If some oil import interruption occurs, a lack of transportation capacity will make it difficult to reallocate large quantities of domestic oil from these relatively oil abundant regions to the East Coast. Thus residents of the East Coast, who have borne a disproportionate share of the cost of oil import controls, will also bear a disproportionate share of the costs of any import interruption.[20]

A second deficiency is that (between 1966 and 1973) the East Coast's imports of residual fuel oil were exempt from significant import restrictions. In 1972 imports of residual fuel oil were about 1.7 million barrels per day; daily crude oil imports were actually less—only 1.5 million barrels. Two consequences of this exemption have been to lead to the "export" of refinery capacity (primarily to the Caribbean) and to reduce the flexibility of the domestic economy for dealing with possible supply interruptions.[21] Both consequences reduce U.S. oil security. Both could have been avoided if the U.S. had never permitted residual fuel oil imports but had instead permitted East Coast refineries to import an equivalent amount of crude oil.

A third deficiency of the mandatory oil import control policy was its failure to recognize and take account of the fact that not all imported oil was equally insecure. For example, oil from Canada must be regarded as more secure than oil from any OPEC country.

Also, within OPEC, Indonesia and perhaps Nigeria presently appear to be more responsible oil suppliers. A wiser oil import policy would have sought to discriminate in favor of such suppliers.

In sum, between 1970 and 1973 our mandatory oil import control program was a failure, because it failed to achieve a reduction in our dependence on insecure foreign oil but it continued to cause a large and totally unjustified regressive redistribution of income from one identifiable group of citizens—oil consumers—to another—oil landowners, producers, and refiners, and taxpayers of the large oil-producing states.

PRESIDENT NIXON'S NEW OIL IMPORT POLICY

By late 1972 President Nixon recognized that U.S. oil import policy had failed. In his special energy message to the Congress (April 18, 1973), he described this failure, rather vaguely, as follows:

Today . . . we are not producing as much oil as we are using, and we must import ever larger amounts to meet our needs.

As a result, the current Mandatory Oil Import Program is of virtually no benefit any longer. Instead, it has the very real potential of aggravating our supply problems, and it denies us the flexibility we need to deal quickly and efficiently with our import requirements. General dissatisfaction with the program and the apparent need for change has led to uncertainty. Under these conditions there can be little long-range investment planning for new drilling and refinery construction.[22]

In order to remedy this failure the President issued an executive order proclaiming three important changes, effective no later than May 1, 1973.

1. All existing tariffs and quotas on imported crude oil and refined products would be removed.
2. A license-fee quota system would be substituted for the just-abolished tariffs and quotas. Under this system, "present holders of import licenses may import petroleum exempt from fees up to the level of their 1973 quota allocations."[23] However, this exemption will be totally phased out by 1980. Im-

ports in excess of the exempt amount are allowed, but a fee (i.e., tariff) must be paid.

3. In order to encourage the expansion of U.S. refining capacity the license fees on crude oil imports will eventually be 21 cents per barrel (by November 1975) whereas the license fees on *all* refined product imports will be 63 cents per barrel, and companies building or expanding either refineries or petrochemical plants will be allowed to import 75 percent of their additional crude oil inputs without paying the license fee.

The changes proclaimed by President Nixon deserve our applause. They mark a major step forward for U.S. oil import policy. They should stimulate a much-needed resumption of U.S. refinery construction and, by elminating the quota protection for the domestic crude oil producers' market share, should promote greater efficiency in the production of domestic oil.[24] Also, by 1980, elimination of the quota will completely eliminate the ethically suspect gifts of valuable import rights from the government to refiners and petrochemical producers. Nevertheless, the President's reforms are not fully satisfactory because they fail to take advantage of obvious differences in the security of oil supplies from different foreign sources. Part III of this study oulines additional policy reforms aimed at remedying this deficiency.

IS THERE A PETROLEUM CONSPIRACY?

Responding to the public outcries arising from the shortages of refined products plaguing the United States in early 1973, the Permanent Subcommittee on Investigations of the Senate Committee on Government Operations asked the Federal Trade Commission to assess the recurrent charge that "the fuel shortage is a deliberate, conscious contrivance of the major integrated petroleum companies to destroy the independent refiners and marketers, to capture new markets, to increase gasoline prices and to obtain the repeal of environmental protection legislation."[25] In a widely cited report released to the press last July, the FTC expressed its support for this conspiratorial theory.[26] According to the FTC, "the major oil companies in general and the eight largest [integrated] majors in particular have engaged in conduct . . . squeez[ing] independents at both the refining and marketing levels." [27] This ability to squeeze, the FTC goes on to say, "has its origin in the structural peculiarities of the petroleum industry" which allow the majors to "limit effectively the supply of crude oil to a point which reduces refinery profits to zero. Clearly, such a system creates a hazardous existence for independent refiners who have little or no crude production." [28] Finally, making a deduction worthy of such disparate types as Milton Friedman and Ralph Nader, the FTC reasoned that those structural peculiarities unique to the petroleum industry were largely the fault of two pernicious governmental policies: oil import quotas and the oil depletion allowance.

Chapters 6 and 7 establish that the depletion allowance and import quotas have benefited the domestic crude oil industry by subsidizing production and protecting markets. But this fact is not sufficient to establish that the integrated majors could profit by adopting a strategy of squeezing their competitors, the independent refiners. Squeezing could be both profitable and successful only if the majors enjoyed special advantages over their independent competitors. The FTC report mistakenly argues that they enjoyed two.

1. "The import quota clearly contributed to profits earned in producing crude oil by elevating prices, but the quota increased profits to the major in another way. The right to import went only to existing refineries. Thus, the major companies . . . were able to purchase oil at the world price as an input for their refineries, which produced final products at elevated domestic prices.[29]

2. Oil depletion allowances were passed originally as a method of encouraging oil exploration. . . . A crude oil producing firm is permitted to subtract from its gross income before taxes an amount equal to 22 percent of its total revenues from crude production. . . . Under this system the major integrated firms have an incentive to seek high crude prices. The high crude prices are, however, a cost to the major firms' refineries. Thus, an increase in crude prices implies an increase in crude profits but a decrease in refinery profits. The integrated oil companies gain

because the depletion allowance reduces the tax on crude profits, while refinery profits are not subject to the same advantageous depletion deduction.[30]

THE EVIDENCE

Oil Import Quotas

The general rule for allocating the valuable rights to import non-Canadian foreign crude oil was that they be given to domestic refiners as a percentage of their total crude oil inputs. However, the allocation formula was based on a sliding scale that granted small refiners a larger share of permitted imports. Table 7-1 shows the sliding scale formulas applicable in Districts I–IV (all states except those bordering on the Pacific Ocean and Nevada) and District V (the remaining states) in 1969. The sliding scale was applied to each company's aggregate refinery inputs. Thus, it had the effect of giving small refiners a far larger per barrel subsidy. Table 7-4 calculates the value in 1969 of the per-barrel subsidy which the sliding scale awarded three refiners of very different size. It shows that the value of the subsidy received by the nation's largest integrated refiner, Standard Oil of New Jersey, was 5.41 cents per barrel; that received by a medium-size, aggressive Midwestern independent—Clark Oil—was more than twice as high, 13.65 cents-per-barrel; and that received by a small refiner, Husky Oil, was more than five times as high, 28.09 cents per barrel. These results are not atypical. Because of the use of sliding scale formulas, large refiners were systematically awarded far smaller per-barrel subsidies by the United States' mandatory oil import control program. But, this means that the FTC must be wrong when it suggests that the allocation of oil import rights provided the large integrated majors with a tool for squeezing their smaller independent competitors.[31]

Oil Depletion Allowances

The FTC's second charge is that because the oil depletion allowance reduces the effective tax rate applicable to profits earned from

Table 7.3 Sliding Scale Formulae: 1969

Average Barrels per Day of an Oil Refiner's Crude Oil Inputs	Allowable Imports as a Percent of an Oil Refiner's Crude Oil Inputs	
	Districts I–IV	District V
0–10,000	19.5	40.0
10–30,000	11.0	9.3
30–100,000	7.0	4.1
100,000 +	3.0	1.9

SOURCE: U.S. Cabinet Task Force on Oil Import Control, *The Oil Import Question* (Washington: G P.O., 1970), p. 12.

Table 7.4 Per Barrel Subsidies Awarded to Three Oil Refiners in 1969 [a]

Firm	1 Daily Total Crude Oil Input [b]	2 Daily Total Crude Oil Imports Allowed by Sliding Scale	3 Gross Value of Daily Import Rights [c]	4 Per Barrel Subsidy to Refiner [d]
Standard Oil of New Jersey	992,000 barrels	35,810 barrels	$53,715	5.41 ¢
Clark Oil	97,651 barrels	8,886 barrels	$13,329	13.65 ¢
Husky Oil	11,000 barrels	2,060 barrels	$ 3,090	28.09 ¢

[a] These calculations are intended to be illustrative only. They are premised on two simplifying assumptions: 1) The refineries of all three firms are located in Districts I–IV. 2) None of these firms was claiming "historical" import rights.

[b] Estimates of daily crude oil inputs are obtained from Moody's. These are approximations.

[c] The right to import one barrel of oil into Districts I–IV was worth about $1.50 in 1969 (see *The Oil Import Question*). Thus the product of $1.50 times the daily crude oil imports allowed yields the gross value of import rights.

[d] Obtained by dividing column three by column one.

the sale of crude oil, the large integrated majors have raised the price of crude oil and thereby diverted taxable profits from their refining operations to their crude oil operations. As a result, the FTC continued, squeezing of independent refiners has been an obvious consequence. This charge, although it sounds plausible, is nevertheless flawed. It is easy to demonstrate, using the FTC's own data, that 16 of the 17 largest integrated majors would find adoption of the alleged profit-shifting tactic unprofitable.

The FTC's analysis makes two mistakes. The first arises from its failure to properly take account of the fact that most of the integrated majors are not self-sufficient. That is, to operate their U.S. refineries at desired levels they had to buy some oil from independent producers of U.S. crude. Other things being equal, a rise in the price paid for crude oil bought from others must mean reduced profits for any given integrated company. This serves to reduce their profit potential from raising crude prices. The FTC's second mistake stems from its failure to take any account of the fact that producers of most domestic crude oil pay royalties and severance taxes on any oil they produce. Within the U.S., crude oil royalties (paid to the oil land's owner) nearly always range between 12.5 percent and 16.67 percent of the gross wellhead price; severance taxes (paid to the state in which the oil is produced) typically range between 2 and 5 percent of the gross wellhead price. Because of the need to pay both royalties and severance taxes, more than 15 percent of any rise in gross pre-tax revenues from a specified crude oil operation will not be reaped by its producer. Thus, the net effect of royalties and severance taxes is to offset roughly three-quarters of the tax reduction granted to crude oil producers by the depletion allowance.[32]

If one takes account of the two factors just discussed, one can easily show that the profit-shifting strategy suspected by the FTC would only yield higher profits for those integrated companies able to produce at least 93 percent of their crude oil needs (see footnote for proof).[33] Table 7-5 reproduces the FTC's estimates of crude oil self-sufficiency for the 17 largest integrated American refiners in 1969.[34] Except for Getty Oil, only the sixteenth largest, none of these integrated giants produced more than 93 percent of its total domestic needs. Hence, none enjoyed enough crude oil self-sufficiency for the profit-shifting tactic, which the FTC claims was practiced, to be profitable.[35] The after-tax losses because any of these firms adopted this strategy would have ranged from a low of 3 cents on each dollar of profits shifted by relatively oil-rich Marathon Oil to a high of 48.3 cents on each dollar of profits shifted by relatively oil-poor Standard Oil of Ohio.[36] These costs are so high that profit-shifting by these 16 integrated majors must be viewed as implausible.

The present shortage of refined petroleum products is not the result of a petroleum conspiracy. Instead, it is the result of a vari-

Table 7.5 The FTC's Estimates of the
Domestic Self-sufficiency of 17 Leading
Refiners in 1969 *

Company	Self Sufficiency (Percent of runs to stills)
Standard (New Jersey)	87.4
Standard (Indiana)	50.5 [a]
Texaco	81.0 [b]
Shell	62.1
Standard (California)	68.8 [a]
Mobil	42.2 [c]
Gulf	87.6 [a,d]
ARCO	64.9
Sun	46.7 [e]
Union	64.3 [a]
Standard (Ohio)	6.7 [a]
Phillips	51.8 [a]
Ashland [f]	12.6
Continental	64.0
Cities Service	49.9
Getty [g]	137.2 [d]
Marathon	88.1

SOURCE: *Preliminary Federal Trade Commission Staff Report on Its Investigation of the Petroleum Industry* (July 1973), p. 20.

[a] Other liquids included in crude production.

[b] Estimated.

[c] Other liquids included in refinery runs.

[d] Excludes crude processed for company's account.

[e] Crude production includes Canada.

[f] 12 months to September 30, 1969.

[g] Includes subsidiaries.

ety of pedestrian factors that either stimulated our demands for refined petroleum products or discouraged additions to our supply. If they are to be solved, the United States' four energy problems require immediate and constant attention. One reason they have received neither is that concern with the politically popular conspiracy charge has diverted public attention from both these very real problems and the failure of existing policies allegedly designed to remedy them.[37] A comprehensive and effective energy policy will be possible only when both the public and the government admit that our energy problems are not due to the machinations of a few giant oil companies.

8.

NATURAL GAS
POLICIES

Crude oil and natural gas are frequently found and produced together; some natural gas is nearly always dissolved in crude oil and many crude oil fields have natural gas caps. Until the 1920s much of the natural gas produced in "association" with crude oil was thought to be an undesirable by-product; it had to be separated from the crude prior to refining and, because of its high transportation costs per Btu, could not be sold profitably. Thus, it was a customary production practice for natural gas produced in association with crude oil to be separated and either reinjected into the reservoir or flared at the wellhead.

In the 1920s use of large-diameter pipelines was found to greatly reduce the costs of transporting natural gas. Acting upon this knowledge, pipelines began to be laid between the major gas fields in Louisiana and Texas and the large population centers in the Midwest and on the two coasts. Depression and war slowed this construction, but it spurted once again after World War II.

Since the close of World War II, natural gas has been the United States' fastest growing major energy source: it satisfied about one-eighth of total U.S. energy demands in 1945; in 1972 it satisfied roughly one-third. The key to this Cinderella transformation was the steep reduction in the delivered price of natural gas because large new pipelines allowed even larger reductions in gas transmission costs. In addition to transportation economies, the switch to natural gas has been accelerated because relative to its principal competitors—coal and crude oil—its wellhead price was low, and it is an especially desirable fuel for processes where clean combustion is desirable.

When pollution control became a major goal of U.S. energy policy in the late 1960s, clean-burning natural gas was recognized as our most desirable fossil fuel. Unfortunately, domestic output is no longer sufficient to meet even current demands: natural gas supplies are now severely rationed; millions of customers have been denied the option of purchasing natural gas. The next section examines the prologue of what is now a familiar story: that the chief cause of our current natural gas shortage has been Supreme Court decisions forcing the Federal Power Commission (FPC) to regulate natural gas wellhead prices. Also, there is an evaluation of the economic and distributional consequences of the FPC's present wellhead price regulations. Policy options are discussed at the end of this chapter.

FPC WELLHEAD PRICE REGULATION [1]

The Natural Gas Act of 1938 authorized the Federal Power Commission to regulate interstate pipelines in order to "protect consumers against exploitation at the hands of the natural gas [pipeline] companies." [2]

This was thought to be necessary because of the "great economic power of the pipeline companies as compared with that of communities seeking natural gas." [3] Since the interstate gas pipelines did (and do) enjoy tremendous scale economies, protection of their consumers from possible monopoly exploitation was (and is) a valid policy goal.

The scope of the 1938 Act was ambiguous. Until the early 1950s the FPC maintained that this act did not empower it to regulate the prices pipelines paid gas producers; instead, the Commission held that it only justified application of traditional rate-of-return utility price regulation to interstate pipeline operations. The FPC rationalized this decision by appealing to the theory that, since producers of natural gas were competitive, the price paid by its ultimate consumers could be satisfactorily controlled by regulating the tariffs interstate pipelines could charge.

As long as natural gas wellhead prices stayed near their Depression levels, there was no consumer opposition to the FPC's ruling that the Natural Gas Act did not authorize their regulation. This consumer indifference evaporated quickly after the rapid expansion of interstate pipeline capacity led to huge postwar increases in natural gas demand. As demand increased, so did the wellhead price of natural gas. Consumer representatives reacted to these higher prices by asking the FPC to reverse its decision not to control them. Two justifications were offered. Most frequently heard (initially) was the justification that such price controls were necessary because "there was monopoly control of the in-ground gas, and . . . the pipeline buyers paid higher-than-competitive prices for restricted amounts of gas." [4] In the Phillips decision (1954), the Supreme Court implicitly accepted this justification and ruled that the Natural Gas Act of 1938 required the FPC to regulate wellhead prices.[5] Many economists have challenged the facts used by the Court to justify its Phillips verdict. Most persuasive is Paul Mac-Avoy's empirical study, *Price Formation in Natural Gas Fields*. MacAvoy shows that the wellhead price increases of the 1940s and 1950s were due both to rising demand and the entry of new natural gas pipelines (i.e., buyers) into the major natural gas fields. Thus, he concludes:

> Regulation is generally conceded to be of doubtful propriety if the reasons for imposition of controls were fallacious. Regulation was advocated in the courts and Congress to prevent monopoly prices in the Southwest. Studies of most field and supply markets in Texas, Louisiana, Oklahoma, etc., indicate the presence of systematic competition or monopsony throughout the period in which regulation was proposed. The problem to be solved by regulation seems not to have existed, so that the court mandate was given for "wrong" reasons. The necessity for Federal Power Commission regulation is doubtful.[6]

The second justification for FPC regulation of natural gas wellhead prices is easily summarized: Because the supply of natural gas is very price-inelastic, sharply higher prices would not lead to appreciably higher outputs; instead, their chief consequence would be ethically suspect income transfers from consumers to owners and producers of natural gas. Commenting favorably on this rationale for natural gas wellhead price regulation, one economist wrote:

> The truth is that we accept regulation . . . where inelasticities and the resulting possibility of windfall income . . . to producers pass the limits of political tolerance. . . . Reduced to its simplest terms, the issue is whether Mr. Getty shall buy a yacht . . . or whether thousands of New Jersey commuters shall enjoy an extra evening "on the town" in Manhattan once a year.[7]

The inference that large wealth transfers are the principal consequence of higher natural gas prices is premised on the factual assumption that natural gas supplies are very price-inelastic. Is this assumption correct?

In addition to recognizing that natural gas (like crude oil) comes from sources with large geologic variations in size and productivity, the assumption that its supply is price-inelastic was initially justified by the following tail-can't-wag-the-dog argument: Crude oil and natural gas are frequently joint products. However, in most cases where they are produced together, the market value of crude oil is many times higher than the market value of natural gas. Thus, all other things being unchanged, any given rise in the price of natural gas would lead to a far smaller proportionate rise in the total revenues expected from a petroleum company's joint oil and gas operations. In turn, this reduces the responsiveness of natural gas supplies to natural gas price changes.

The large natural gas producing companies have rebutted the above argument by asserting that the "dilution" effect is minimal. They support this assertion by pointing out that presently nonassociated gas (i.e., gas not produced in conjunction with crude oil) accounts for about 90 percent of total supplies. The revenue-raising effects of a gas price rise are not diluted for producers of nonassociated gas. This rebuttal also requires qualification. It is true that if a field is currently producing nonassociated gas, then, other things being equal, a given percentage gas price rise will lead to a proportionate rise in field revenues. However, because roughly half of all nonassociated gas appears to be discovered by exploratory wells actually aimed at finding oil, firms in the process of searching for new oil or gas supplies do not expect to enjoy a proportionate rise in revenues (as a result of a given gas price rise) if their search proves successful.[8] For the reasons summarized in our discussion of the tail-can't-wag-the-dog argument, this can reduce sharply the price incentive to search for new gas supplies. The possible long-run importance of this qualification is indicated by the following observation:

> From the longrun point of view, the key factor in the supply of gas is the new field discovery. The supply curve of new field gas is the counterpart of the conventional longrun supply curve. In practice, new field discoveries play the same rejuvenating role that the replacement of old machines by new ones plays; it may be possible to get by without replacement, but not for a long time. . . . In thinking, therefore, of the longrun adequacy of supply, special consideration should be given to . . . the new field discovery. . . . Qualitatively, one Mcf of new field gas discovery is not the same as one Mcf of gas extensions. For gas supply, new field supplies are the trunk of the tree without which new branches cannot grow.[9]

The true price-elasticity of natural gas supply ought to be somewhere between what the optimists (i.e., gas producers) and pessimists (i.e., gas consumers) believe. This knowledge is of little help to the policymaker because neither optimists nor pessimists have furnished firm, quantitative evidence of the elasticity of natural gas supplies. Unfortunately, the empirical evidence offered by academics who have studied this industry is also unsatisfactory.[10] In sum, we have little quantitative knowledge about the long-run price-elasticity of natural gas supply. Thus, any projections of the magnitude of any wealth transfers because of a natural gas price rise should be regarded as highly speculative. The uncertainty of the magnitude of such wealth transfers weakens the "prevents undesirable wealth transfers" rationale for the FPC's regulation of natural gas wellhead prices. The following analysis of the consequences of the regulations promulgated by the FPC shows that this rationalization is further weakened because present policies, besides being very inefficient, actually result in ethically questionable income transfers.

The FPC initially attempted to carry out the Supreme Court's mandate in the Phillips decision by regulating the thousands of natural gas producers on an individual cost-of-service basis.[11] This resulted in its being swamped with paperwork. However, it did not lead to the result consumer interests sought—a freeze on wellhead prices—because

The Federal Power Commission refused to review initial price on a new contract . . . but it did review price later . . . when an . . . increase was requested. This left producers and buyers free to sell new reserves for unregulated prices, since control of prices could be avoided by paying a higher initial price.[12]

Because demand continued to soar throughout the 1950s and competition was replacing monopsony in the markets where natural gas was sold to pipelines, natural gas wellhead prices nearly doubled between 1954 and 1959.[13] When presented with the fact that wellhead price rises had not stopped after its Phillips decision, the Supreme Court ruled in the CATCO case (1959) that the FPC's wellhead price regulation procedures were inadequate.[14] The FPC responded to both the CATCO decision and its unbearable paperwork load by adopting area-wide wellhead price regulation in September 1960.

To implement area-wide price regulation, the FPC divided the country into its major gas-producing regions. Then, rather than attempting to decide the permissible prices on an individual gas field basis, it attempted to establish a uniform ceiling price for gas from all fields in an area. This price was set at a level equal to that area's average production costs. Within each area this price applied to gas reserves that cost different amounts to produce and that had different values to their consumers because of either location or size advantage.[15] Individual companies were allowed to make contracts with any available buyers at any price at or below the regulated ceiling price for that area.

Within the general framework just outlined, the FPC initially developed a two-price system which it proposed to follow pending completion of formal area rate proceedings:

For each designated geographic area, the FPC set two guideline prices. One price—the higher figure—represented the top price that the commission would regard as permissible in deciding whether to certificate a new sale. The other marked the price level to which the commission would refer in deciding whether to suspend a price increase filed pursuant to an existing contract. . . . It appears that the price for new sales was based on the highest price at which sales in the area had been previously certificated and the "suspension" price determined by reference to the weighted average price for all sales in the area. These prices . . . were, in short, a means of establishing a "freeze"—albeit one subject to modifications—while formal proceedings were going forward. Their practical effect, however, has been marked. Prices in all of the producing areas have remained relatively stable throughout the last decade [i.e., the 1960s].[16]

Since 1960 the FPC has conducted several area rate proceedings. Because of likely differences in the price-elasticities of different types of gas, the multitiered price system has been retained. For example, the Southern Louisiana proceedings (1968), accounting for about one-third of all gas sold in interstate commerce, established a three-tiered price system. So-called "first vintage prices" fixed ceilings on both associated gas and "old" gas sold under pre-1961 contracts; "second vintage prices" fixed a one cent Mcf (thousand cubic feet) higher ceiling on all sales of nonassociated gas consummated between January 1, 1961 and October 1, 1968; "third vintage prices" raised the ceiling an additional one-half cent per Mcf on all subsequent sales of nonassociated gas. Because these, and subsequent liberalized price ceilings, have been far below the level necessary either to elicit large increases in natural gas supply or to significantly reduce the ever-growing level of demand, the natural gas shortage has worsened.

ECONOMIC AND DISTRIBUTIONAL CONSEQUENCES OF FPC WELLHEAD PRICE REGULATION

The area-wide wellhead price ceilings set by the FPC have reaped a plethora of adverse consequences. It is informative to discuss these under three general headings: traditional efficiency and equity problems arising from the enforcement of any price ceilings that lie below the market clearing price, efficiency problems arising from the price-setting procedure actually used by the FPC, and special problems arising because intrastate gas sales are exempted from the price ceilings.

*Efficiency and Equity Problems Arising from the
Enforcement of any Price Ceilings that Lie
Below the Market Clearing Price*

Economists define a product as being in short supply whenever the quantity demanded exceeds the supply. Given this definition, product shortages are impossible unless a product's price is constrained from rising to its market clearing level. If for any reason the market clearing price is thought to be too high, price ceilings are a tool that the government can use to prevent prices from rising to this level. Unfortunately, because it gives rise to shortages, use of this tool is not costless.

If asked to analyze the economic and distributional consequences of the "successful" implementation of a price ceiling policy for natural gas, the good student of introductiory economics might offer the following analysis: Suppose the demand and supply curves for natural gas are as shown in Figure 8-1. Then, in the absence of any price ceiling, the market will be cleared (i.e., $D = S$) when Q_E units are sold at price P_E. This solution is said to be economically efficient in the sense that gas consumers value the last unit consumed as just equal to its cost. Because the value of all other units consumed actually exceeds their cost, consumers reap a net gain from their consumption. Even though it is economically efficient, the government may not judge this market-clearing solution desirable because of the distributional consequences stemming from a high gas price. For example, suppose the government concludes that price P_E is "unfairly" high because natural gas land owners and producers collect huge rents—totalling $P_E ABC$—from consumers. It could reduce these rents to any "justifiable" amount by selecting the appropriate price ceiling. Suppose P_1 is declared to be that ceiling. Then, consumers' rental payments do fall to $P_1 DBC$. But, at this price, Q_1 units are

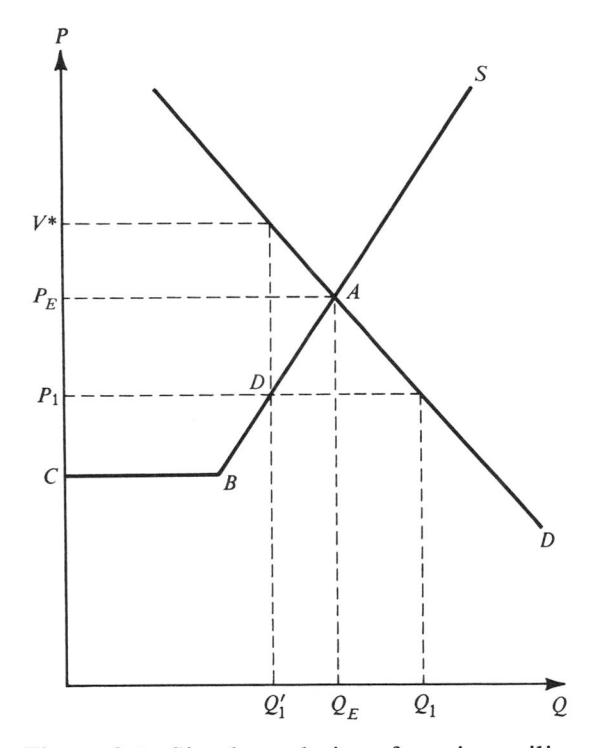

Figure 8-1. Simple analytics of a price ceiling
on natural gas' wellhead price.

demanded and only Q_1' are supplied—there is a shortage of gas.
Because prices are constrained from fully performing their allocation function, some type of nonprice rationing is required.

The redistribution of income (wealth) from natural gas suppliers
to consumers is the alleged benefit from wellhead price ceilings.
Clearly these ceilings benefit that subset of consumers who can
continue to buy all of the gas they desire—they pay less. Just as
clearly, they hurt natural gas suppliers. However, in addition to
suppliers, another party is hurt: those citizens who are unable to
get all (or frequently any) of the gas they desire and could obtain if
gas prices were allowed to rise to the market clearing level, P_E. It
is easy to show that the monetary loss suffered by both the suppliers and excluded consumers must exceed the monetary gain

reaped by those consumers fortunate enough to be able to buy lower cost gas.[17]

The losses suffered by the excluded consumers would be larger the more price-inelastic their gas demand and the more price-elastic the natural gas supply. Because of insufficient empirical evidence, quantitative estimates of these losses are not provided. Nevertheless, two factors prompt me to conclude that they have undoubtedly grown sharply over time:

1. The long-run supply of natural gas is much more price-elastic (in the relevant output range) than the short-run supply, because it takes time for firms to increase their exploration and development expenditures in order to find and develop new gas supplies. Even though gas demand was growing at about 5 percent per year, the number of gas wells completed in 1971 was only 73 percent of the number completed in 1960 (i.e., 3830 v. 5258).[18] This suggests that, since 1960, gas producers have found it far less profitable to take steps to increase gas supplies. Increasingly lower (in real dollars) gas price ceilings offer a simple explanation for this otherwise paradoxical behavior.

2. Because of the continued failure of new gas supplies to grow as fast as demand, shortages of natural gas have grown progressively worse over the past few years. As a result, rationing has become more stringent. For example, in the mid-1960s, when gas shortages were slight, buyers of interruptible gas supplies were the chief victims of any necessary rationing. Presumably, since they chose to buy interruptible service, the gas demands of most of these customers were relatively price-elastic. Hence, the costs they bore because of gas rationing should not have been very high. Buyers of interruptible gas service remain one of the chief victims of gas rationing. However, since the late 1960s, another rationing device has been increasingly used—the blanket refusal to provide service for broad classes of potential gas customers. The bitter protests by those denied service reflects the fact that many have price-inelastic gas demands.

To summarize, the FPC's enforcement of stringent wellhead price ceilings has led to a growing shortage of natural gas. As time passes, and the shortage worsens, it becomes less likely that the "social" valuation of the monetary gains reaped by those consumers who can obtain all (or most) of the gas they desire at the low ceiling price offsets the "social" valuation of the monetary losses suffered by gas suppliers and those consumers denied gas service. The date has long since passed when the income redistribution argument provides a valid justification for the FPC's wellhead price regulation.

Efficiency Problems Resulting from the FPC's Price-Setting Procedures.

One of the proclaimed goals of almost all regulations is to encourage efficient production. Efficient production of any product requires that an industry produce those units having the lowest delivered cost. For two reasons, the way in which the FPC sets area-wide price ceilings makes efficient production of natural gas impossible.

Gas is most valuable if found in fields that are large or close to market. The fact that the FPC's area-wide wellhead price ceilings do not accurately reflect either intra- or interarea "valuation" differences is one cause of productive inefficiency. The analytics of the problem can be best shown by a discussion of a hypothetical example. Suppose residents of a city can buy gas from two sources located in a neighboring state. One is located next to the city gas company; gas transport costs are zero. The other is located 50 miles away, but in the same FPC rate setting area; gas transport charges to the city's gas company are 10 cents per Mcf. Other things being equal, the gas company would be willing to pay 10 cents per Mcf more for "local" gas. Suppose the FPC sets the area-wide wellhead price ceiling at 20 cents per Mcf. Then, no higher-cost gas would be produced. That this would be wasteful can be readily demonstrated by assuming that all of the "local" gas costs more than 20 cents but less than 30 cents to produce. Then, none of this gas would be produced even though its delivered cost is less than that for gas produced in the more distant field.

The different area price ceilings allowed by the FPC were initially (and continue to be) based on the prices paid in each area just prior to the FPC's announcement of its regulations in 1960. There were rather large interarea differences in these ceilings. To the extent that these reflect interarea "valuation" differences stemming from location, etc., the bad efficiency effects just discussed are mitigated. Unfortunately, MacAvoy's study confirms that a large part of these interarea differences can be explained instead by the fact that the gas pipeline companies exercised far stronger monopsony power in some areas (usually the low-price ones) than they did in others.[19] Enforcing lower prices in those areas where monopsony was strongest accentuates the economic inefficiency.

The multitiered price ceilings, which keep prices for "old" and "associated" natural gas below those received from sales of "new" gas, also make the production of natural gas less efficient. Since supplies of "old" and "associated" gas probably are less price-elastic than supplies of "new" gas, these differential ceilings have been justified by the distributional argument summarized earlier.[20] Nevertheless, since operating and gathering costs must be incurred whenever any natural gas is produced, and since these tend to rise over time as the gas reserves in any given field are depleted, supplies of "old" and "associated" gas cannot be perfectly price-inelastic. Thus, enforcement of the multitiered price system must reduce production of "old" and "associated" gas below the level that would be profitable if its price were allowed to rise as high as the price allowed for new gas. Failure to produce this gas is economically wasteful.

Problems because Intrastate Gas Sales Are Exempted from the FPC's Wellhead Price Ceilings

Intrastate sales of natural gas are exempt from FPC wellhead price regulation. Since gas producers prefer to sell their output at the highest possible price—but only those customers within the state can pay more than the FPC ceilings—wellhead price regulation has caused supplies of gas available for intrastate sale to be artificially high. This is economically inefficient because (1) it has caused migration of large gas consumers (who would otherwise prefer to locate in another state) to the large gas-producing states, and within these states it is profitable to use gas in some ways (e.g., petrochemical feedstocks and boiler fuel) which from a national viewpoint must be regarded as wasteful. It should be emphasized that the distortions arising because intrastate gas sales are exempted from FPC regulation will become more severe (hence, costly) as the difference between the market clearing price and the ceiling price widens.

POLICY OPTIONS

The above arguments confirm that the FPC's wellhead price regulation has failed. This failure has been recognized by both a majority of the current FPC commissioners and President Nixon.[21] There are two basic ways to correct it: have Congress pass legislation abolishing all (or most) regulation of natural gas wellhead prices or keep the wellhead price regulations (perhaps making some modest reforms) and instead develop new supplemental gas sources. Unless Congress acts, the FPC must choose the second alternative.

We shall next evaluate the most promising supplemental gas sources and show that the elimination of all natural gas wellhead price regulation is, at this time, the preferable policy option. The United States' worsening gas shortage could be alleviated by developing large supplemental sources of supply. The supplemental sources most frequently mentioned are pipeline shipments from northwestern Canada and the Alaskan North Slope, synthetic gas (SNG) made from crude oil, or other more exotic hydrocarbon sources (e.g., oil shale, tar sands, or garbage), and imports of liquified natural gas (LNG). High cost is the chief problem plaguing gas supplies from supplemental sources: Gas from the Alaskan North Slope or northwestern Canada will cost at least $1.00 per Mcf just to transport to the U.S. border. Both crude oil and coal cost more than twice as much (per Btu) as "new" interstate sales of natural gas. Thus, SNG made from either coal or crude oil will have to cost several times more than "new" gas. Presently it is not known whether large-scale commercial production of SNG made from other more exotic sources is technically feasible. (3) It now appears that large imports of liquefied natural gas from Algeria or the Soviet Union will cost about $1.50 per Mcf.[22] These costs compare unfavorably with the representative 26 cents per Mcf wellhead price currently received for "new" interstate sales of Gulf Coast natural gas.

In addition to being far more expensive than domestically produced natural gas, gas from most of these supplemental sources is less desirable because its supply is either less secure or environmental damage is an inevitable by-product of its production and transportation. Specifically, implementation of the proposals to import LNG from Algeria and the Soviet Union or to make SNG from imported crude oil would seriously reduce the security of U.S. energy supplies. Implementation of the proposals to ship Arctic gas via pipeline over the permafrost to U.S. markets or to strip mine more coal in order to produce SNG would have obvious adverse environmental consequences.

In sum, as long as supplies of "new" natural gas from domestic sources remain cheaper, more secure, and environmentally preferable to gas supplied from any supplemental sources, the U.S. ought to take steps to encourage its production. Abolishing most FPC wellhead price regulations would have this desirable consequence.[23] Unfortunately, because Congress faces strong pressure from consumers to keep gas prices from rising, legislation abolishing FPC wellhead price regulation remains unlikely.

"ROLLING-IN"

Natural gas pipelines pay different prices for equally valuable supplies of gas. For example, gas bought in the mid-1950s under a standard 20-year contract costs roughly half as much as current purchases of "new" gas from the same field. "Rolling-in" refers to the interstate pipeline practice of selling gas to local distributors at a price (exclusive of pipeline tariffs) just equal to its average cost. Because natural gas prices have gradually risen, its rolled-in price must be less than its current marginal cost.

Rolling-in is economically inefficient because it encourages the consumption of gas in uses that yield net benefits less than its real costs. Nevertheless, since pipeline companies make their profits on gas transportation and not from the sagacious purchase and sale of gas supplies, they prefer to roll-in prices, thus encouraging greater gas consumption and larger pipeline revenues. They justify this practice by arguing that it would be inequitable to charge different classes of gas consumers different prices solely because members of one class are fortunate enough to be able to buy gas from a "cheaper" source. As a practical matter, as long as the difference between the average price that the pipeline pays for gas and the price that it pays for "new" gas is not very large, the decision as to whether rolling-in is permitted or denied is not of major importance. This has been the case until recently. Thus, the fact that the FPC allowed pipeline companies to roll-in prices aroused little public opposition.

A proposal by El Paso Natural Gas to import large quantities of Algerian LNG at 80 cents per Mcf kindled new interest in this debate precisely because the differences between rolled-in and non-rolled-in prices will be huge. El Paso suggested two reasons why it should be allowed to roll-in prices. First, it would be inequitable to charge those customers "unfortunate" enough to receive the Algerian LNG more than twice as much for their natural gas. Secondly, if rolling-in is not allowed, El Paso would not be able to sell anything like the large quantities of LNG it had planned to import and which are necessary if the project is to be economically feasible. Critics of rolling-in have seized upon El Paso's second reason by noting that it implies that the net benefits from consuming much of this imported LNG must indeed be less than its cost. In order to forestall the use of natural gas from such costly supplemental sources, they advocate that rolling-in be disallowed.

There would be no rolling-in problem if all wellhead price controls for natural gas were abolished; natural gas prices would rise to the level of marginal costs. However, as long as wellhead price ceilings are enforced, the FPC must adopt some policy on the rolling-in question. If forced to choose between allowing or denying rolling-in, I would prefer that the FPC choose the latter in order to discourage development of socially wasteful (i.e., expensive) supplemental gas sources. However, a third policy alternative might be preferable to both. This policy would force the pipeline companies to use rolled-in pricing, but then the U.S. government would place a tax on each Mcf sold. This tax would be set to just equal the difference between the price that any pipeline pays for gas from its highest cost source and its rolled-in price. This policy is preferable to rolled-in pricing because it is economically efficient—every gas consumer pays a price equal to its marginal cost. It is preferable to non-rolled-in pricing when evaluated according to distributional criteria because the government (i.e., taxpayers) rather than a subset of fortunate gas consumers is the beneficiary of any income transfer.

9.

OTHER POLICIES

This chapter examines a potpourri of other policies affecting energy demand or supply: two policies that will play a key role in determining future levels of oil and gas transportation costs—"Jones" Act-type regulation of tanker operations and federal policy towards "superport" construction; the present and likely near-future effect on petroleum demand and supply of recent attempts to control emissions of air pollutants from both stationary and mobile sources; thumbnail sketches of problems likely to arise if we accelerate our development of new energy supplies from coal and nuclear power.

THE JONES ACT

In order to provide the United States with "a merchant marine of the best equipped and most suitable types of vessels sufficient to carry the greater portion of its commerce and serve as a naval or military auxiliary in time of war or national emergency" Congress passed the Jones Act in 1920.[1] This act provides that "no merchandise shall be transported by water . . . between points in the United States . . . in any other vessel than . . . [one] . . . built in and documented under the laws of the United States and owned by persons who are citizens of the United States. . . ."[2]

The Jones Act was designed to strengthen the merchant marine by prohibiting foreign competition on all intercoastal runs. Unfortunately, once freed from the need to meet the prices of their foreign competitors, American crews, shipbuilders, shipowners, etc. succeeded in raising the prices of their respective services. As a result, it quickly became a rule of thumb that shipments on U.S.-flag vessels cost roughly twice as much as shipments on foreign-flag vessels.[3] Faced with these higher ocean-transport costs, consumers of American-flag shipping began to search for substitutes; their success in finding them is shown by the nearly continuous decline in the relative size and quality of the American merchant marine since the Jones Act's passage in 1920.

Enforcement of the Jones Act raises the annual costs of transporting oil from Texas and Louisiana to the U.S. East Coast by at least $100 million.[4] Since this act has had a deleterious effect on the strength of the U.S. merchant marine and since there is no other good reason for annually transferring over $100 million from oil consumers to domestic shipping interests, the entire rise in petroleum transportation costs must be considered a social waste. This waste can be alleviated by abolishing the Jones Act, but this is unlikely. Instead, it is far more likely that the beneficiaries of the current act will succeed in their unremitting efforts to persuade Congress that its deficiencies can be remedied by reforms designed to extend its coverage. In 1972 a bill that would require 50 percent of all oil imported in the United States to be carried on U.S.-flag carriers came very close to passage. If this "reform" had been in force during 1972, U.S. oil importers would have paid an additional $198 million for foreign oil.[5]

Enhancing national security and protecting the environment provide the principal justifications for proposals to extend the coverage of the Jones Act.[6] Briefly summarized, the national security justification holds that since the U.S. is becoming much more dependent on insecure foreign oil, it should take steps to insure against becoming dependent on foreign tanker fleets for the transportation of this oil. That is, the U.S. should seek to avoid dual dependency. That dual dependency should further exacerbate our already difficult oil import security problems is assumed by all proponents of legislation designed to extend the Jones Act. Why it should do so has never been explained.

Representatives of oil companies and of consumer groups have rebutted this nebulous security argument for extending the Jones Act's coverage by pointing out that even though the ships they own or lease for long-term charter are not under U.S. registry, many have been classified by the Department of Defense as being under "effective U.S. control." [7] This designation was adopted by the Joint Chiefs of Staff in 1947–48. It only applies to ships owned by U.S. interests and registered under the laws of Liberia, Panama, and Honduras. Even for these ships the classification is not automatic; as of January 1, 1971 only 74 percent of the American-owned tanker tonnage registered under these three foreign flags was classified by the Defense Department as under effective U.S. control.

The backers of an extension of the U.S. flag requirements to ships carrying our oil imports counter this rebuttal with the argument that effective control is inadequate. They assert that the political views of the country of registry are more persuasive than those of the country of ownership. They document this assertion by citing examples where American-owned vessels registered under foreign flags have refused to transport cargoes (including oil) to or from such strategically vital areas as South Vietnam or the Middle East; in addition, they cite instances where such ships have participated in trade with Cuba and North Vietnam.

Testimony in recent House hearings revealed that most of the examples cited of foreign flag ships acting contrary to U.S. security interests did not involve ships classified by the Defense Department as being under effective U.S. control. [8] Indeed, when attention is focused on ships so classified, there are only two examples of them acting in contrary ways. The first involved an unescorted Liberian tanker that refused to enter the Gulf of Aqaba during the 1967 Arab-Israeli war, despite U.S. insistence on the right of free passage. This refusal occurred after the tanker had suffered twelve hits, from an unidentified vessel, while attempting passage through the Straits of Tiran. Presumably if this had happened in the context of a national emergency or war directly involving the U.S., this tanker would have received a protective escort from U.S. naval forces.

The second example involves vessels classified as under effective U.S. control but allowed by their countries of registry to trade with Cuba and North Vietnam. What backers of a Jones Act extension fail to note is that as soon as the United States imposed sanctions on trade with these countries, all ships classified by the Defense Department as under effective U.S. control ceased trading with them. In sum, there is no merit to the security argument for an extension of the Jones Act to ships delivering imported oil.

The environmental protection justification for requiring greater use of U.S. flag tankers holds that the government can achieve large reductions in pollution by enforcing stricter standards for ship construction, maintenance, and operations. This justification rests on the implicit—and suspect—assumption that the United States is powerless to exercise similar controls over foreign-flag ships entering its ports. Existing pollution-control statutes apply with equal force to all tankers currently entering U.S. waters.[9] One already authorizes the government to impose a maritime lien of up to $14 million to cover the actual costs of removal of discharged oil.[10] Having gone this far, it is apparent that Congress could also require all vessels entering U.S. waters to meet any ship construction, maintenance, or operating standards that it deemed appropriate. In sum, because mechanisms already exist for achieving both the security and environmental goals discussed above, and since their enforcement will not result in the ethically suspect transfers of additional millions from oil importers and consumers to the oil-shipping interests, any extension of U.S.-flag requirements to tankers delivering foreign oil deserves opposition.

SUPERTANKERS AND SUPERPORTS

Because of the huge scale economies in tanker transportation, the size and composition of the world tanker fleet has undergone dramatic transformation over the last decade.[11]

In the . . . five years from 1965 to 1970, the number of ships in the world fleet with capacities in excess of 100,000 deadweight tons (dwt) increased from 19 to 319. Before this decade ends . . . their number should easily exceed 1000. By then, the 200,000–300,000 dwt tanker and combination-bulk carrier will become the standard workhorses of the world bulk trade.[12]

The supertanker revolution has led to sharp reductions in the costs of transporting crude oil. Unfortunately, the revolution has by-passed the United States. According to a study prepared for President Nixon's 1973 energy message, "there are at least 60 ports or buoy facilities currently in operation worldwide which are capable of handling ships of 175,000 deadweight tons or more."[13] None are located in the U.S. As late as 1960 none of the major European and Japanese ports were large enough to handle the 60,000 dwt tankers that then (as now) dock at the major East and Gulf Coast ports. When these other large oil-consuming nations began to expand their ports to service supersized vessels in the early 1960s, why didn't the U.S. choose to do likewise? The two most likely explanations are economic: First, scale economies in tanker transportation are largest when oil is shipped long distances.[14] Most oil for European and Japanese consumption came from Persian Gulf sources tens of thousands of miles away. In contrast, until recently, almost all oil consumed in the United States came from Western Hemisphere sources at most only 2000 to 3000 miles from their final U.S. markets. Secondly, since the Jones Act doubled the costs of shipping U.S.-produced oil via tanker, the oil industry decided that it was more profitable to expand the nation's pipeline networks than to expand the size of its ports and U.S.-flag fleet.

Recently the U.S. has begun to import much larger quantities of oil from the Persian Gulf, 24,000 miles away. Moreover, our consumption of this oil must rise rapidly over the next few years. Recognizing this fact—and its corollary that the inability to use supertankers raises oil transportation costs sharply—the American oil industry is now in the forefront of the battle to persuade the U.S. government to permit construction of one or more superports on the East and Gulf Coasts. President Nixon has also endorsed the construction of superports; however, some environmental groups remain opposed. Since there is no question that superports are desirable when judged solely by economic criteria, our task is to assess the environmental case against them.[15]

Fear of large oil spills provides the principal environmental argument against constructing superports. However, some also oppose them for more aesthetic reasons—they dislike growing port congestion and industrialization.[16] This aesthetic argument is something of a red herring because far fewer supertankers will be required to deliver any specified quantity of oil in the future.

Some of the immediate effects of oil spills—especially large spills close to shore—are well known. The fouling of beaches and killing of sea birds are documented by recent experience. In addition to the immediate destruction, an oil spill also has residual destructive effects. After most of the lighter petroleum fractions have been vaporized, there remains a lumpy, tarlike residue which can foul marine plant life and pollute beaches. In some intertidal areas, concentrations of these inert hydrocarbons have already reached dangerously high levels in the shellfish that feed upon oil-fouled plant life. It should be emphasized, however, that the environmental damage of a given-sized oil spill is greatly reduced if it takes place at sea. "After oil is spilled it releases most of its toxic properties within 24 to 72 hours by evaporation and dissolution. If the oil does not reach the biologically productive shore areas for 72 hours, major ecological damage is averted." [17]

The pollution resulting from tanker operations consists of two types: accidental pollution due to groundings, collision, or mismanagement of valves and deliberate operational pollution due to engine room waste and tank washing. While spectacular accidents like the sinking of the *Torrey Canyon* attract the most public attention, deliberate releases account for as much as 1.5 million tons of oil pollution each year.[18] In fact, tank washings, a normal operating procedure on all tankers, probably account for more oil pollution than any other single factor.[19] Replacement of conventional tankers with supertankers should not lead to an increase in this type of deliberate pollution. Thus, the mere fact of its existence does not offer an argument against the United States building superports.

Port congestion is a major cause of collisions and groundings.[20] Over the last 10 years, 80 percent of all tanker accidents have occurred when ships entered or left ports. Hence, the replacement of conventional tankers with supertankers ought to reduce port congestion. Unfortunately, compared with conventionally sized tankers, supertankers are much more difficult to stop and maneuver, and require much deeper drafts. Vast amounts of dredging would be required to deepen and widen any of our existing East or Gulf Coast ports. Dredging on such a large scale threatens to destroy ecologically valuable tidal marshes and to allow intrusion of saltwater into coastal freshwater supplies. Moreover, in the event of a supertanker accident, enormous environmental damage would occur because huge quantities of oil are released into ecologically fragile intertidal port areas. Authorities agree that the best way to avoid these problems is to build new superport facilities offshore.

Two basic types of offshore port facilities are possible: mooring buoys and artificial islands. The oil industry backs single- or multipoint moorings; i.e., one or more buoys connected to onshore storage areas by a pipeline buried beneath the seabed. These are favored because they are cheaper than any alternative and could be built in one or two years. For example, in 1973 a consortium of oil companies proposed building a $67 million Gulf Coast terminal, construction would take two years and the initial throughput would be 1.7 million barrels per day.[21]

As of mid-1973 the Corps of Engineers and the Maritime Administration appeared to favor the second alternative: construction of one or two huge offshore islands to service both the East and Gulf Coasts. Estimates are that each artificial island would cost about $1.3 billion; even after its construction was authorized, a project of this magnitude would take several years to complete.[22] Moreover, a large fraction of the oil shipped to these artificial islands would have to be transshipped to distant coastal ports by smaller tankers.

The sole environmental advantage of the artificial island is that barriers may be placed around a berthed vessel to contain any oil spills. "At a single point mooring bouy, the ship would swing with the current and the wind making containment barriers impractical." [23] This environmental benefit of artificial islands is more than offset by the fact that most major oil spills do not take place when tankers are unloading but when they are navigating congested waters. Because several tankers will be unloading at the artificial islands at any specified time and because extensive transshipment by smaller tankers to conventional ports will be required, some collisions seem inevitable. Single point mooring buoys will not be plagued by these congestion problems. Since they are also much cheaper to build and operate, this is the type of superport facility our government should require.

MANDATORY EMISSION STANDARDS

Responding to the American public's growing perception of and concern with air pollution, Congress passed the 1970 amendments to the Clean Air Act "to speed up, expand and intensify the war against air pollution." [24] The regulations promulgated under the authority of the 1970 amendments impose mandatory standards for air emissions from both stationary and mobile sources.

The stationary source emission standards were designed to sharply reduce the amounts of sulphur oxides, nitrogen oxides, and particulates dumped into the atmosphere by large energy-consuming industries such as electricity generation and metal smelting. Each state has been required to draw up "primary air quality standards—those related to health—that must be met by 1975 while more stringent secondary standards—those related to the 'general welfare'—must be met within a reasonable period." [25]

The stationary standards approved by the Environmental Protection Agency (EPA) attempt to control sulphur oxide emissions in two ways. First, they limit the sulphur content of any fuel burned; secondly, they limit the amount of sulphur oxides that can be discharged into the atmosphere. Developed reserves of both natural gas and low-sulphur coal are already in short supply, and technological problems are delaying the commercial introduction of devices for "scrubbing" emissions from the combustion of high-sulphur coal. Thus, President Nixon was moved to observe:

If we insisted upon meeting both primary and secondary clean air standards by 1975, we could prevent the use of up to 155 million tons of coal per year. This would force an increase in demand for oil of 1.6 million barrels per day. This oil would have to be imported. . . .

If, on the other hand, we carry out the provisions of the Clean Air Act in a judicious manner, carefully meeting the primary, health related standards, but not moving in a precipitous way toward meeting the secondary standards, then we should be able to use virtually all of that coal which would otherwise go unused.[26]

Faced with this evidence, the President strongly endorsed the EPA's recent decision not to enforce the secondary standards in 1975. In view of our severe near-term shortage of secure crude oil and natural gas, this policy decision deserves endorsement.

The motor vehicle emission standards require 90 to 95 percent reductions in the levels of emissions of carbon monoxide, hydrocarbons, and nitrogen oxides. These strict standards for carbon monoxide and hydrocarbon emissions are now scheduled to be enforced beginning in the model year 1976. Enforcement of the nitrogen oxide standards is scheduled to commence one year later.

The automobile companies' efforts to reduce production of these three pollutants have been plagued by a technological dilemma: [27] Both carbon monoxide and hydrocarbon emissions are most easily reduced by raising combustion temperatures; unfortunately, more smog-causing nitrogen oxides are produced when combustion temperatures are higher. Even at this late date, the actual commercial technology the automobile manufacturers will use to circumvent this dilemma remains uncertain. The American companies have been moving toward the adoption of a dual-catalyst vehicle that, according to a study of the prestigious National Academy of Sciences, will raise automobile sticker prices $270 above 1973 levels and will cause them to consume 25 percent more fuel than their 1970 counterparts.[28] Honda, a Japanese manufacturer of motorcycles and automobiles, has introduced a stratified charge engine that satisfies the carbon monoxide and hydrocarbon standards and promises to meet the nitrogen oxide standards. The National Academy of Sciences believes that adoption of this much more durable engine would raise sticker prices by less than $100 and not lead to any fuel diseconomies.[29] Unfortunately, the stratified charge engine may not be available in sufficiently large numbers by 1976. Thus, a delay in the enforcement of the mandatory air emission standards is desirable. Otherwise, automobile companies would be

forced to "tool up" their assembly lines to produce far less satisfactory dual-catalyst vehicles.

COAL

Faced with rapidly worsening shortages of secure crude oil and
natural gas, U.S. energy policymakers have begun to press for
increased reliance on two alternative energy sources: coal and
atomic energy. This section and the next will explain why it is
unwise to emphasize them with regard to solving our present and
anticipated near-term energy shortage.[30]

Coal is by far the most plentiful type of fossil fuel available in
the United States, known remaining coal reserves have been estimated, with a high degree of certainty, at over 3.2 trillion tons.
Moreover, there is widespread consensus that more than half of
these reserves are recoverable without major technological innovations.[31] Unfortunately, when compared to oil and gas, relative
abundance of domestic supplies is the *only* virtue that can be
claimed for coal. Thus, one investigator of the coal industry
writes:

> My work on coal has involved continued discovery of its enormous and
> growing drawbacks. It is hard to imagine how one fuel can have so many
> disadvantages [compared] to its competitors. Actually, all these problems
> seem to be reflections of one proposition—coal is a solid fuel containing
> large proportions of impurities. This makes coal harder to mine, trans-
> port, process, and use. Solidarity also has proved to have increased coal's
> environmental problems.[32]

What are these problems? Are they severe enough to eliminate reliance on increasing coal supplies as a substitute for oil and natural
gas?

Unless it is first converted into synthetic crude oil or natural gas,
coal cannot be burned in internal combustion engines, is highly
inefficient for space heating, and is too "dirty" to be used in most
industrial processes. Because of these well-known deficiencies,
coal's share of our total energy supply has been falling for over 40
years. Because a technological breakthrough that would permit
sharp reductions in the costs of producing commercial quantities of

synthetic oil or gas from coal seems unlikely in the near future, even backers of policies designed to encourage coal's increased utilization concede that significant inroads are possible in the near future only in electric power generation.

According to the President's Office of Emergency Preparedness—an enthusiastic proponent of increased coal utilization—adoption of all feasible policies to increase the electricity generating industry's coal-burning capacity would result in an additional oil savings of at most 2.5 million barrels per day in 1980.[33] Since electric utilities have not voluntarily chosen to adopt OEP's strategy of substituting coal for fuel oil, we know that it has been more expensive. The cost of steam coal sold east of the Mississippi rose roughly 66 percent between 1969 and 1972.[34] Part of these higher costs are attributable to new, but long overdue, requirements for installation of mine safety equipment and changes in production practices mandated by the Mine and Health Saving Act of 1969. In addition, they also reflect a worsening shortage of low-sulphur coal. Eastern utilities, faced with these higher coal costs (whatever the cause), opted to expand by building either new oil- or nuclear-fired generating capacity.

Compared to its competitors in the market for fueling electricity generating plants, Western coal has remained relatively cheap. Unfortunately, this coal is located long distances from our major electricity consumption centers and, because of its relatively low-energy content, is more expensive to transport than its Eastern counterpart. In view of these higher transport costs, accelerated development of huge mine mouth generating plants presently offers the only economical way to use large new quantities of this coal. Since costs also limit the distances electricity can be commercially transmitted, increased emphasis on this energy source would not result in appreciable decreases in our reliance on oil and gas in the absence of new public policies specifically designed to achieve this goal.

In view of the growing insecurity of our crude oil supplies, that coal is more expensive than other currently available energy sources does not provide sufficient evidence for concluding that the United States should not adopt policies designed to encourage increased reliance on it. High environmental costs that would result from such increased consumption must also be considered. These are of two types: the destruction of vast land areas because of strip mining and the poisoning of our atmosphere with sharply increased emissions of particulates and SO_2.

Experience with large-scale strip mining in the Appalachian region has conclusively demonstrated its adverse environmental impact in hilly areas. They include massive water pollution from sedimentation, landslides, destruction of scenic views, etc.[35] While reclamation can alleviate many of the water pollution and landslide problems, it cannot restore the land to anything resembling its natural state:

Perhaps the most noticeable effect of strip mining is aesthetic. The sylvan grace and green charm of Appalachia has been deeply scarred by the highly visible white bands encircling its hills on as many as five levels; the red, orange or yellow streams and the large spoil piles. While mountains have been defaced, decapped or leveled in the name of cheap coal.[36]

This unavoidable and permanent environmental damage is much more horrible than the potential damage from the increase in offshore drilling for the oil and gas that would be necessary to supply equivalent amounts of additional secure energy.[37]

In addition to destroying the aesthetic qualities of vast areas of land, increased coal combustion must also lead to a sharp rise in particulate and SO_2 emissions. The SO_2 problem promises to be especially severe in the populous East because most Eastern coals have high sulphur contents and there is still no commercial technology for scrubbing most of this poison from power plants' flue stacks. Western coal is blessed with a low sulphur content. Unfortunately, it has such a high ash content that its combustion results in a noticeable rise in particulate emissions.

In sum, coal has especially bad air-polluting properties. The Congressional decision to force the EPA to pass regulations severely limiting emissions of these pollutants attests to their high social costs. In view of these costs and the availability of other secure and cheaper sources of lower-polluting energy, the recent emphasis on developing our coal supplies seems unwise. Over at least the next 15 years it would be much wiser to take steps encouraging greater oil and gas flows from Alaska, Canada, and the offshore areas (including the Atlantic Coast).

NUCLEAR POWER

Since World War II, nuclear power has been vociferously proclaimed as the energy of the future. Faced with worsening shortages of "secure" fossil fuels, proponents of nuclear power are contending that "the future is now." Because it takes seven to nine years before a newly commissioned nuclear-power electrical generating plant can be operational, accelerated development of nuclear power cannot possibly alleviate our energy supply problems during the 1970s. The key problem facing our policymakers is whether accelerated development of nuclear power should be backed as one way to alleviate the worsening energy shortages projected for the 1980s.[38]

The United States had 29 commercial nuclear power plants in operation at the end of January 1973; they were producing roughly 4 percent of our total electricity output. In addition, 57 plants were being built and 76 were in the planning stage. Present projections are that 20 percent of the United States' total electricity needs will be generated by nuclear plants in 1980.

There are two types of nuclear fission power plants: light water reactors and liquid metal fast breeder reactors.[39] Light water reactors are presently the only type in use; the Atomic Energy Commission expects that the breeder reactor will be operating commercially in the mid-1980s. The AEC views light water reactors as stopgap plants differing from the "superior" breeder in two important ways: (1) The light water reactor utilizes about 1 percent of the energy content of uranium as compared to about 70 percent for the breeder. (2) Because it is cooled by liquid sodium rather than water, the breeder can operate at much higher temperatures than the light water reactor; this results in higher thermal efficiencies and less thermal pollution. In fact, the thermal pollution from breeder reactors would be less than from new fossil fuel plants.

When producing electricity, nuclear power is superior to fossil fuels in several ways. First, "nuclear power plants do not emit particulates, sulphur oxides, or other combustion products." [40] Thus, air pollution by electric utilities would cease to be a problem if nuclear power plants were used. Second, in many regions of the country, electricity produced from new nuclear plants is cheaper than that produced from new fossil fuel plants.[41] In addition to the fall in the price of uranium 235 over the same period when prices for fossil fuels have risen, nuclear power's improved comparative costs can be attributed to technological developments permitting the use of slightly rather than highly enriched nuclear fuels and the development of extremely large pressure vessels which have resulted in large-scale economies arising from increased reactor size. Third, substitution of nuclear power for fossil fuels (especially coal) will lead to a reduction in water pollution, land disruption, and the loss of life that are the by-products of conventional fossil fuel mining practices. Finally, because the breeder reactor will produce more fissionable material than it consumes, its development would assure a virtually inexhaustible fuel supply. In turn, this would allow us to use our scarce reserves of secure low-polluting fossil fuels for purposes other than the generation of electricity. In sum, increased substitution of nuclear power for fossil fuels promises to yield substantial benefits. But what are the costs?

Increased use of nuclear power will give rise to four types of costs. First, because of their low thermal efficiency, thermal pollution is a serious problem with light water reactors. Because cooling towers already provide a commercially feasible solution to this problem, it should be given little weight.

A more important cost of nuclear power is the need to find safe methods by which to dispose of radioactive wastes. Spent fuel is withdrawn annually from reactors for reprocessing. This involves dissolving the solid enriched uranium fuel element in concentrated acid solutions and removing any still-valuable materials for further use. Chemicals are also used to sort the remaining radioactive wastes into short- and long-lived products. Short-lived wastes are simply set aside and allowed to decay. Long-lived wastes are further subdivided according to the danger they pose to human life. Most dangerous are "high-level" wastes such as strontium 90 and cesium 137; these will remain dangerous for over 1000 years. About 3 million barrels of high-level wastes are already stored in large underground steel tanks. Because of corrosion, these tanks must be replaced every 20 years.[42] Presently the AEC is considering a promising permanent solution to this problem: to convert the liquid wastes into solids and store these in steel drums placed on the floor of a dry geological formation; salt placed between these drums would be heated by the wastes' radioactive decay to a semimolten state, and after the canisters corroded away, the wastes would be permanently encased in a tomb of salt. Because such sophisticated waste-disposal schemes seem likely to be commercially feasible in the relatively near future, I find the verdict rendered by two scientists who have studied the nuclear waste-disposal problem persuasive:

> In public discussion of nuclear power and public safety, much concern is expressed about the need for storing the radioactive wastes for centuries. While such long-term storage is an essential part of nuclear power development, the projected public safety issue involved is minimal, compared with other environmental problems.[43]

A third cost of the proliferation of nuclear power plants is the need to prevent stealing of fissionable materials. One possible scenario involves a blackmail threat in which a large sum of money and the reversal of specified policies is demanded of a president in return for which a designated target will be spared nuclear holocaust. Because knowledge about how to construct atomic bombs is widely known, such a hellish scenario is possible if a terrorist group can acquire a relatively small quantity of either highly enriched uranium 233 or plutonium. Fortunately, production of either of these products is so expensive as to be beyond the means of any conceivable domestic group; moreover, if attempted, detection is likely. Unfortunately, uranium 233 will be used as a fuel in breeder reactors and plutonium is a by-product of all fission reactors, but especially the breeder. These materials could be stolen from uranium enriching plants, reactors, reprocessing plants, or in transit. Shipments of purified plutonium and uranium 233 from fabrication or reprocessing plants to reactors are thought to be the most likely targets for theft. Presently both products are shipped in two-gallon tanks by rail or on unguarded trucks.[44] One truckload of either is enough to build a score of atomic bombs.

In order to reduce the possibility of nuclear theft, two proposals have been advanced. One, called the "hot atom" approach, would prohibit full purification of plutonium and uranium 233. The purification process would be stopped while the fuel is still sufficiently radioactive to require heavy containers—these would make handling by thieves much more difficult and dangerous. Also, the additional processing costs could easily be beyond the means of any private organization. The second proposal calls for building "nuclear parks" in which enriching plants, reactors, and reprocessing plants would all be built. Such parks could be securely enclosed and protected. However, because a single enriching or reprocessing plant produces enough fuel for a score or more reactors, there is some question as to whether nuclear parks of the requisite size would be commercially feasible.

The fourth and most important cost attributable to the increased use of nuclear power is the possibility of a reactor accident. Such accidents would probably not involve atomic explosions. Rather, radioactivity would be released into the atmosphere and those in its path would suffer radiation maiming and death.

The most likely type of nuclear accident would involve the meltdown of a reactor's radioactive fuel rods. The probable cause of such a meltdown would be a loss of primary coolant due to a clogged pipe or pressure loss. For radiation to be released into the atmosphere, both the inner containment vessel surrounding the nuclear core and the outer containment shell (the familiar domed roof of the reactor) would have to be breached. The outer shell is thought to be fairly secure because any pressure would be dispersed over a large area and it is not subject to continuous radiation exposure. Nevertheless, if, as a result of a meltdown, the nuclear core explodes (this would not be an atomic explosion) fragments could pierce the outer shell, releasing radiation into the atmosphere.

To prevent a meltdown following a loss of coolant, reactors are equipped with emergency core cooling systems designed to flood an overheating core with water long enough for the fuel rods to be removed and the nuclear reaction shut down. The Atomic Energy Commission is not scheduled to complete its test of these cooling systems prior to 1975. By that time, more than 100 reactors will be operating with cooling systems that many scientists outside the AEC regard as suspect.

Because of a near total lack of empirical information, experts disagree sharply in their evaluations of both the probability of such an accident occurring and the costs if it does. However, all appear to agree that a major accident is far more likely if breeder reactors (favored by the AEC) are used.[45] Should a major accident occur near an urban area, the prospect of hundreds of thousands dead and tens of billions in property destroyed must be regarded as a possibility.

When the Atomic Energy Commission was created in 1946 it was assigned the dual role of promoting peaceful applications of nuclear power and of protecting the public interest. Because the influence exercised by the AEC grows larger as the peaceful uses of nuclear power proliferate, there is good reason for suspecting that environmentalists are justified when they assert that these two roles are contradictory and that protection of the public has been given short shrift. Thus, one authority has written:

Both sides think the probability of a major accident is low, but low means different things to different people. In the spectrum of estimates, officials in Washington lead toward lower estimates—on the order of one chance in a billion—than researchers in the laboratories. "What bothers me most," says a prominent engineer at Oak Ridge, "is that after 20 years we are still making purely subjective judgments on what is important and what is not in reactor safety. Purely by decree, some things, like the rupture of a reactor pressure vessel are ruled impossible. To decide these things without some objective measure of probabilities is, to me, almost criminal." [46]

Faced with this enormous uncertainty, it seems prudent to adopt a cautious research-oriented strategy toward atomic energy. Nuclear power should not be counted upon to provide the answer to our energy problems in the 1980s.[47]

III

A NEW ENERGY POLICY

10.

REFORMING EXISTING ENERGY POLICIES

THE FAILURE OF U.S. ENERGY POLICY: RECAPITULATION

The United States consumes 35 percent of the world's energy output, with oil and gas providing three-fourths of the total. U.S. energy consumption may double by 1985, but domestic reserves of petroleum fuels could supply their present share of the projected increase only at sharply higher costs. Large-scale supplies of nuclear energy are more than a decade away and sharp increases in our current level of coal consumption would entail unacceptably high environmental costs.

These capsulized facts show that the fundamental energy problem facing the United States is to secure supplies of low-cost energy sufficient to meet the demands of a growing economy. The problem of adequate supply has two principal dimensions. On the one hand, the "modern Malthusians" argue that continuation of current rates of economic growth threatens to totally exhaust Earth's energy resources within the next 100 years. They predict a cataclysmic decline in both population and industrial production at that time. Chapter 1 assessed this argument and concluded that, at present, it should be of little concern to U.S. energy policymakers.

Chapter 1 gave far more credence to a more immediate energy problem facing the United States: securing adequate supplies of low-cost crude oil and natural gas between now and 1985. During this period, U.S. energy requirements will roughly double and crude oil and natural gas will have to supply 65 to 75 percent of these doubled needs.

The U.S. must rely heavily on oil and gas imports to meet its near-term energy needs. Because we have run out of readily available spare energy capacity and because it would take several years before large new supplies from any domestic source could be developed, a sudden interruption of oil imports would require severe rationing throughout the American economy. Preventing such interruptions or minimizing the costs (including the need to respond with military force), if they occur, is properly regarded as the United States' second energy problem. A realistic evaluation of the actual importance of this "security" problem requires policymakers to assess both the extent and likelihood of oil and gas import interruptions. This was the subject of chapter 2. It concluded that there was a very real possibility of repeated costly interruptions of U.S. oil and gas imports as a result of political or economic decisions b··   eral of the large oil-exporting countries
to d   s their output. Worldwide oil shortages
raeli conflict offer an appetite-ruining
such interruptions can create. Because
s are high, reducing the probability of
goal for the U.S. government.
tates' vital security interests has of-
ariety of federal policies designed to
duction. Unfortunately, higher do-
conflicts with the professed federal
tal pollution. Critics of the Presi-
ction of the trans-Alaskan pipeline
for both crude oil and natural gas
possible environmental damage
the expected security gain. As of
e failed to persuade our political
ption. Nevertheless, they have
it the danger of environmental
tion and distribution of energy

is an important public problem. Consideration of the difficult conceptual and practical problems this raises for energy policymakers provided the grist for chapter 3.

The fourth important energy problem arises because existing policies lead to large income transfers from one group of citizens to another. The term "transfers" denotes a payment for which no productive service is rendered. In the absence of clear public policy justification, governments normally do not sanction policies forcing the transfer of something valuable from one group of citizens to another. Indeed, some top-level U.S. energy policymakers have confessed that such income transfers constitute ethically suspect privileges. Nevertheless, because of the fundamental geological fact that domestic oil and gas comes from a great variety of heterogeneous sources, chapter 4 explained why present oil and gas policies have, on balance, forced American taxpayers and oil consumers to annually transfer several billion dollars to owners of oil lands and residents of the major oil-producing states.

Part I discussed the four important energy problems facing the United States. Part II's five chapters presented a series of case studies of the important public policies aimed at assuaging one or more of them. These established that current policies have failed to solve any of our energy problems. In fact, on balance most have exacerbated them. This failure explains the alarmed cries of "energy crisis." Rather than recite the specific reasons why each of these policies has failed, it is useful to search for more general causes. I believe there are two: the inability or unwillingness to coordinate existing policies and the failure to adopt flexible policies responsive to the ever-changing situations that we face. Discussion of these two causes follows.

U.S. energy policy emanates in bits and pieces from a variety of different power centers. Any list of the most important would include executive departments such as Interior, Commerce, State, Defense, and Treasury, and administrative agencies like the Federal Power Commission, the Environmental Protection Agency, and the Atomic Energy Commission. Within most of the above there are several subpower centers, and all are subject, in varying degrees, to pressure from a plethora of concerned Congressional committees, Presidential assistants, courts, industries, mineral landowners, and, for want of a better term to describe the residuum of interests that remain, "the public." By deliberate design as much as by bureaucratic neglect, each of these power centers sees only a part of the total problem and typically represents only a few of the interests involved. As a result, suboptimization is inevitable. This problem can be solved only by placing someone in charge of coordinating all federal energy policies.

On April 18, 1973, President Nixon responded to this "coordination crisis" by establishing a National Energy Office, whose director (to be appointed by the President)

> . . . shall recommend policies and guidelines pertaining to energy matters for all energy related programs within the Executive Branch. To the maximum extent permitted by law, Federal officers and Federal departments and agencies shall cooperate with the Director in carrying out his functions.[1]

The director was instructed to report to the President through the Special Committee on Energy composed at that time of top Presidential Assistants Kissinger, Shultz, and Watergate victim Ehrlichman. In light of the enormous power possessed by these three aides at the time this order was issued, it seems likely that the President intended this change to be more than cosmetic. Nevertheless, in view of the long-established tradition of power over energy policy held by a great variety of entrenched groups and the sharp erosion of Presidential power because of Watergate, I suspect that it will be a long time before an appreciable change is wrought in the uncoordinated way in which U.S. energy policies are presently made.[2]

The second cause of energy policy failures has been our adoption of inflexible policies that cannot adjust to the inevitable changes in the fundamental "facts" upon which they are based. At any time these facts are ambiguous because of the lack of "hard data" about such important parameters as the long-run price and income elasticities of demand and supply for the major kinds of energy, the speed with which secure domestic energy supplies can be expanded, and the security of energy supplies from different foreign sources. The ambiguity of these facts is directly attributable to the sources of geological, technological, and political uncertainty already described. It will only be alleviated as better knowledge accumulates over time. As the costly failures of such policies as natural gas wellhead price ceilings and mandatory oil import controls illustrate, whenever there is considerable uncertainty about the future status of the industry being regulated, it is poor strategy to adhere blindly to an inflexible policy whose success depends on the occurrence of a specific and unlikely event. Instead, a flexible groping strategy is recommended. Initially a large variety of policy options should be pursued; more resources should, of course, be devoted to those judged most promising. As time passes and we are able to evaluate how well our different policies have worked, the failures should be cut back and at some point eliminated; the successes should receive a growing share of our total resource commitment.

Part II's case studies have already described our most important energy policy failures. At the risk of being repetitious, a description follows of those policies for which there is now ample evidence to justify an irrevocable commitment to their total (but in some cases gradual) elimination. Also examined are those policies which can be fruitfully reformed.

POLICIES DESERVING ABOLITION

Market Demand Prorationing

Prorationing is a precision instrument by which the major oil-producing states have controlled monthly crude oil output. It did help to alleviate the overproduction threatening the American oil industry during the 1930s. However, in the postwar period it became apparent that the remedy was far more costly than the illness it was designed to cure. There were two problems. First, wasteful overdrilling was encouraged because oil fields with deeper and more closely spaced wells were rewarded with higher basic allowables and inefficient high-cost wells were exempted from all prorationing regulations. Secondly, by using prorationing, the large oil-producing states were able to restrict total supply severely, and thereby succeeded in keeping the price of U.S. curde oil far above its competitive level until the mid-1960s. Because of factors discussed in chapter 5, market demand prorationing has recently become a far less offensive policy. However, some costs remain; and if large new domestic oil supplies are ever found in the future, it may again become a noxious policy. In order to foreclose this undesirable possibility, now is the opportune time to pass federal legislation declaring this policy illegal.

Tax Preferences

The American petroleum industry receives two valuable tax preferences: percentage depletion and quick expensing of intangible development costs. Their proclaimed goal is to stimulate increases in domestic production and developed reserves. Percentage depletion is undesirable because it rewards only a small minority of our citizens—chiefly petroleum landowners—and does not lead to an appreciable rise in output or reserves. In contrast, quick expensing of development costs appears to be a relatively efficient way of subsidizing higher domestic petroleum output.

Higher levels of pollution and greater reliance on insecure foreign imports are undesirable by-products of our rising levels of energy consumption. A major cause of our energy crisis is attributable to the fact that the costs of both by-products are not reflected in the price we pay for energy. Energy is too cheap; therefore, our consumption is too high. In light of this fact, any tax subsidy that stimulates even higher petroleum demands by subsidizing production costs must be judged undesirable.

In sum, all petroleum tax preferences—even the efficient ones—ought to be eliminated. However, if they are eliminated immediately, the many millions of stockholders who own petroleum producing companies would suffer rather large capital losses because of the reduction in the after-tax profits reaped from their investments in petroleum production. Because these citizens never really profited from our present tax subsidies—most were shifted to petroleum landowners in the form of higher rents—this loss strikes me as inequitable. In order to reduce the size of this capital loss, Congress could pass legislation ending all preferential tax treatment for petroleum production after a specified number of years (perhaps five). Prior to the date this reform is scheduled to go into effect, the existing tax preferences could be allowed to remain at their current levels. Delaying implementation would reduce considerably the magnitude of the capital losses suffered by present petroleum investors. Moreover, announcing that the reforms would go into effect on a specified date means that prudent investors would suffer no additional losses prior to that time.

FPC Wellhead Price Regulation of Interstate Sales of Natural Gas

Price regulation has led to widespread shortages of this most desirable type of energy and to its socially inefficient overconsumption as boiler fuel in the large gas-producing states of Texas and Louisiana. Both wastes could be eliminated if Congress would enact President Nixon's proposed legislation exempting from all wellhead price regulation "gas from new wells, gas newly-dedicated to interstate markets, and the continuing production of natural gas from expired natural gas contracts." [3] Because most of our current gas production is sold under 20-year contracts, the President appears to be right in asserting that deregulation's immediate effect on most consumers' gas costs would be slight.

Jones Act

Jones Act-type laws require the shipment of goods destined for American consumption on U.S.-flag ships. Enhancing our national security and protecting the environment are the principal justifications offered for these costly laws. Chapter 9 concluded that both justifications are invalid. Thus, legislation repealing the Jones Act would be desirable. In order to make such legislation politically more acceptable, it might be prudent to delay its date of implementation for several years.

POLICIES REQUIRING REFORM

Rents on Public Lands

Combinations of royalties and lease bonuses are used to collect the rents on public lands where commercial quantities of petroleum are thought likely. Because it raises the petroleum producer's costs, this method of collecting petroleum land rents restricts his output below the economically efficient level; however, it does permit shifting from the oil producer to the oil land's owner some of the risk that a particular project will prove unsuccessful. The replacement of the current method of collecting rents by some variant of the two-part lease bonus described in chapter 5 would also permit any desired amount of risk-shifting from producer to landowner but without giving rise to the inefficient reduction of output. Thus, it would be desirable if some such scheme were adopted.

Outer Continental Shelf

Roughly half of the Continental United States' remaining petroleum reserves are thought to lie on the federally owned Outer Continental Shelf. Because of its relative abundance, it seems likely that, on average, this offshore petroleum will be less expensive to produce than the onshore reserves.[4] To spur production of this oil, President Nixon directed the Secretary of Interior to triple the annual acreage leased on the Outer Continental Shelf by 1979. He estimates that this will result in an additional 4 million barrels per day of domestically produced crude oil and an annual increment of 5 trillion cubic feet in natural gas supplies. These estimates are very speculative. Nevertheless, for the reasons summarized below, the President's new offshore petroleum policy is commendable.

Since the Santa Barbara blowout, the public has reacted with hostility to increased offshore drilling. This reaction is based on an exaggerated perception of the likely incidence and magnitude of oil spills from offshore production. As the repeated references to the Santa Barbara spill (and no other) indicate, large spills occur infrequently.[5] Moreover, when they do occur the damage is almost never more than $10 to $20 million. When compared with the high and frequently permanent environmental and safety costs that will be by-products of our production of equivalent amounts of domestic energy from coal, oil shale, or atomic energy, increased offshore drilling is a desirable option.[6]

Oil Import Policy

President Nixon's recent executive order substituting tariffs for mandatory quotas is a major advance for U.S. oil import policy. The new Nixon policy will stimulate a much-needed resumption of U.S. refinery construction and, by eliminating the quota-protection for domestic crude oil producers' market share, should promote greater competition and efficiency. Also, the eventual total elimination of the quota will eliminate completely the ethically suspect gifts of valuable import rights from the government to refiners and petrochemical producers. The chief deficiency of the President's oil import reforms is their failure to exploit the use of the prospect of sharply higher oil imports from a *particular* country as a "carrot" to persuade that country to provide special assurances that its oil exports to the U.S. will not be interrupted. For OPEC members, such assurances might include an agreement to spend or invest in the U.S. a large fraction (perhaps greater than one) of all receipts from the sale of oil to the U.S. and a provision by the exporting nation to store a specified fraction of its annual sales to the U.S. within our borders. Diminution of OPEC's economic and political power would be a valuable joint product of all such assurances.

A low-cost policy that may persuade some oil exporters to offer effective guarantees that their oil shipments to the U.S. will not be interrupted would be to divide countries exporting oil to the U.S. into two classes, secure and insecure, according to explicit published criteria, and then to place a high (perhaps $5.00 per barrel) additional tariff on oil imports from insecure sources. Besides encouraging increased exports by Canada and, perhaps, Indonesia—the only foreign sources that at this writing deserve to be regarded as secure—this policy might enourage potentially large oil exporters not to join OPEC and may even persuade some of

OPEC's present members (e.g., Iran or Nigeria) to consider offering assurances like those suggested above. The prospect that this policy would succeed would be enhanced if other large oil-importing countries (especially the Common Market members and Japan) could be persuaded to adopt a similar strategy.

Offshore Superports

The construction of offshore superports would permit large reductions in the costs of transporting Persian Gulf oil to the U.S. and would reduce both the risks of spills due to collisions and groundings and the damage if they occur. In April 1973 the President proposed legislation to permit the Interior Department to issue licenses allowing superport construction beyond the three-mile limit. Assuming that appropriate environmental standards must be satisfied before a license is issued, this proposal deserves our approval.

Two basic types of offshore port facilities are possible: mooring buoys connected to onshore storage areas by pipelines or elaborate artificial islands from which oil would be transhipped to the coast by both smaller tankers and pipelines. Because mooring buoys are much cheaper, could be built much more quickly, and will be less congested than artificial islands, the Interior Department should be instructed to ignore the preferences of those "empire builders" in the Corps of Engineers and the Maritime Administration who favor the artificial island.

Air Pollution Standards

Brief delays in enforcing the air quality and motor vehicle emission standards presently mandated for the mid-1970s would not result in an appreciable deterioration of our environment. Such delays would permit rather large reductions in both oil imports (perhaps 3.5 million barrels per day) and, it now appears, in the costs of alleviating that part of the air pollution problem attributable to the automobile. Legislation should be passed delaying enforcement of post-1973 motor vehicle emission standards until 1978 and delaying enforcement of the secondary air quality standards until 1980, or even later.

Atomic Energy

The speedy commercial introduction of the liquid metal fast breeder reactor has been and remains the government's highest priority. Obviously, faster development of atomic power would reduce our dependence on fossil fuel; moreover, it would reduce our production of undesirable air pollutants. Nevertheless, in light of the potentially severe and as yet unsolved problems of preventing both nuclear theft and accidents, the too-speedy commercial introduction of this power source could cause a new energy crisis. Thus, the Atomic Energy Commission should be instructed to halt its advocacy of the commercial breeder reactor program until adequate research on safety and antitheft controls has been done. At this time it is unwise to regard atomic energy as the answer to our intermediate-run problem of providing sufficient energy supplies.

EVALUATION OF PROPOSED
ENERGY POLICY CHANGES

Table 10-1 summarizes each of the energy policy changes recommended. The five criteria by which each of these proposed changes was judged are its effects on (1) economic efficiency, (2) net U.S. supply (i.e., total U.S. petroleum demand minus total U.S. supply from all sources), (3) U.S. national security, (4) pollution control, and (5) changes in the magnitude and distribution of any petroleum-based rents. For the first four "objective" criteria, Table 10-1 records unambiguous improvement over the status quo with a plus sign; a minus sign denotes the converse. In addition to noting the mass of desirable plus signs, four comments can be made:

First, adoption of most of these policy changes will raise the economic efficiency of the American petroleum industry; none should lower it. Thus, on balance, adoption of these changes should result in both lower petroleum prices and higher profits for petroleum producers. Publicity of this fact would raise the chances of most of these reforms being adopted.

Secondly, even though the "objective" (i.e., nonincome dis-

Table 10-1 Evaluation of Proposed Energy Policy Reforms

Policy Reforms	Economic Efficiency	Net Supply	National Security	Pollution	Income Distribution
		Criteria for Evaluating Energy Policy			
Abolish prorationing	+	+	+	+	Raise petroleum land rents
Abolish tax preferences	+	−	−	+	Lower petroleum land rents; temporarily reduce producers' after-tax profits
Abolish regulation of natural gas wellhead prices	+	+	+	+	Raise petroleum land rents; raise energy costs of current gas consumers; reduce costs of new gas consumers
Abolish Jones Act	+				Lower rents received by shipping interests
Two-part lease bonus rent-collection procedure from public lands	+	+	+		Raise petroleum land rents
Speedier development of Outer Continental Shelf	+	+	+	+	Raise government's petroleum land rents
Oil import tariff levels differing according to security of source			+		
Offshore superports (mooring buoys)	+	−	+	+	
Delay enforcement of air pollution standards	+	+	+	−	
Slow down development of commercial nuclear power		−	+	+	

tribution) goals of U.S. energy policy appear to be diverse, Table 10-1 shows that adoption of most of these policy changes would advance all of them. In the three instances where unanimity is lacking, the benefits seem to outweigh the costs.

Third, the effect of these policy changes on the magnitude and distribution of petroleum-based rents is mixed. However, on balance, petroleum landowners appear to gain. Thus, while it would be politically impossible to eliminate all existing petroleum tax preferences if this were the government's only policy goal, such an elimination might become possible if this concession were demanded as the price for other policies (especially abolishing natural gas wellhead price regulation and enforcing oil import tariffs) that would lead to sharply higher land rents.

Fourth, it would be most desirable if the whole package of reforms summarized in Table 10-1 were adopted in the near future. However, if this is not possible, partial adoption of this "package" should yield desirable results.

In sum, adoption of this proposed package of energy policy reforms would help to alleviate all of our energy problems. Unfortunately, our energy problems have become so severe that even this drastic set of reforms is not enough. Unless we wish to repeat past mistakes and rely on a fortuitous chain of events to solve our problems, bold new policies are needed.

11.

NEW POLICIES

If the policy reforms outlined in the previous chapter had been adopted just a few years ago, the United States would not now be in the midst of an energy crisis. Unfortunately, because past misguided policies actually tended to accelerate the erosion of our oil security, it is unlikely that even this extensive package of reforms can suffice to surmount our present crisis. Thus, if they are not prohibitively expensive, new policies directly aimed at reducing the insecurity of our energy supplies are also necessary. Since the possibility that exports of OPEC oil will be interrupted is the chief threat to our security, the most likely targets for these new policies are to reduce this ever-present danger directly by checking and if possible destroying OPEC's monopoly power and to reduce the costs resulting from any import interruption by taking steps either to reduce our energy demands and thereby lower our reliance on OPEC oil or to build up our emergency spare capacity. The second approach is analogous to purchasing an insurance policy. However, in this instance, the purchase of "insurance" yields an additional benefit because by reducing the likelihood of success for any specified OPEC embargo threat, it renders all such threats less potent.

CHECKING OPEC'S MONOPOLY POWER

If the OPEC nations had not succeeded in establishing monopoly control over the non-Communist world's supplies of low-cost crude oil, the United States would not face a credible threat to the security of its oil supplies. Thus, if they are neither prohibitively expensive nor risky, policies aimed at lessening OPEC's monopoly are desirable. In chapter 10 I suggested that one low-risk and low-cost policy reform should diminish OPEC's monopoly: charging a sharply higher tariff on oil and gas imports from "insecure" sources. This section discusses two new policies aimed at achieving the same goal.

Formation of a petroleum importers' counter-cartel to conduct all business negotiations with OPEC is viewed by many including some within the U.S. government, as the best way to limit OPEC's power. Supporters justify this policy by noting that if the large oil importers act as a unit they would possess enormous economic power in dealing with OPEC—after all, they ask, who else can buy OPEC's oil? They believe that the jointly made threat to withhold patronage would effectively limit OPEC's price-raising powers. There are three reasons for advising against this policy. The most important is that OPEC would, quite properly, recognize that this counter-cartel threatens its very existence. Faced with such a direct threat, OPEC's managing directors would be derelict if they did not take strong and immediate measures to destroy the nascent counter-cartel. Barring military intervention, OPEC would probably win the resulting battle of the titans because even a brief interruption in the flow of OPEC oil threatens to impose huge costs on most of the industrialized oil-importing nations, whereas the principal OPEC members would suffer little or no discomfort from such an interruption because they possess huge reserves of foreign exchange.

The second fault with the proposed counter-cartel is that it is likely to be unstable. The oil-importing nations have varying interests because of differences in the extent to which they rely on OPEC's oil. In just a few years, after large quantities of oil start to be exported by some of the large North Sea producers, these differences should widen. Historical evidence suggests that when the members' goals are divergent, cartels tend to be short-lived.

A third fault is that the need to use administrative procedures that guarantee an adequate accounting of the diverse interests of the cartel's membership will render its decision-making process both inflexible and slow. Besides dooming the counter-cartel to a dinosaur-like existence, the use of this cumbersome administrative machinery may actually reduce competition among OPEC members because it will make it nearly impossible for individual importers to bargain for "special deals": "distress sales" and the like. Also, by forcing the large multinational oil companies to act in unison, there is little doubt that any monopoly power possessed by these companies will be enhanced.[1]

These three reasons indicate that establishment of an oil importers' counter-cartel is an undesirable and probably futile way to attack OPEC. A much more attractive counteraction is offered by M. A. Adelman's suggestion that the United States government take steps to encourage the multinational oil companies to get out of the business of marketing OPEC oil. Adelman's analysis is best summarized in his own words:

> The producing nations cannot fix prices without using the multinational companies. All price-fixing cartels must either control output or detect and prevent individual price reductions, which would erode the price down toward the competitive level. The OPEC . . . [royalty] system ac
> complishes this simply and efficiently. Every important OPEC
> publishes its . . . [royalties] per barrel: they are a public re
> sible to falsify much. Outright suppression would be
> cheating. Once the . . . [royalties] are set . . .
> [royalties]-plus-cost is safe, and the floor ca
> time, as in early 1971, or early 1972.
>
> It is essential for the cartel tha
> _marketers_, paying the . . .
> to sell it as products
>
> Were the producin,
> in cash or oil for thei.
> price would then be no
> The producing nations w

Otherwise, they would inevitably chisel and bring prices down by selling incremental amounts at discount prices. Each seller nation would be forced to chisel to retain markets because it could no longer be assured of the collaboration of all the other sellers. Every cartel has in time been destroyed by one then some members chiselling and cheating; without the instrument of the multinational companies . . . OPEC would be an ordinary cartel. . . .

Chiselling will accelerate if national companies go "downstream" into refining and marketing. One can transfer oil to downstream subsidiaries or partners at high f.o.b. prices, but with fictitious low tanker rates or generous delivery credits. The producing nation can put up most of the money or take a minority participating, or lend at less than market interest rates. One can arrange buy-back deals, barter deals, and exchange of crude in one part of the world for availability elsewhere. The world oil cartel in the 1930's was eroded by this kind of piecemeal competition, and so will the new cartel of the 1970's if the individual producing nations become the sellers of oil.[2]

Adelman's conclusion that getting the multinational oil companies out of the business of marketing OPEC oil will stimulate more competition is persuasive. Moreover, because most OPEC members are clamoring for increased "participation" rights in the production of their oil, adoption of his proposal should not promote a dangerous direct confrontation between OPEC and the importing nations—OPEC would most likely view this type of policy change as a long-overdue concession. However, at this point, the concluding cautionary note of chapter 2 deserves repetition. OPEC, today, is an immensely powerful cartel—perhaps the strongest in history. This reduces the likelihood that any OPEC-destroying policy will work.[3] Defensive policies, designed to reduce our reliance on OPEC oil, are also necessary.

STOCKPILING EMERGENCY RESERVES

Because it is likely that any attempts to control or destroy OPEC's monopoly power will fail, it is wise to consider buying "insurance." All insurance policies must work by reducing our reliance on insecure energy. In addition to raising domestic supplies—the goal of many of the policy reforms recommended in chapter 10—this end can be achieved by stockpiling emergency reserves and decreasing domestic demands.[4]

Stockpiling of emergency petroleum reserves promises to yield two benefits. It reduces the probability that OPEC will find it "profitable" to interrupt oil shipments, and it reduces the costs if any interruption should occur. The costs of this policy depend on both per-barrel storage costs and the quantity of oil needing to be stored. Writing in 1967, Adelman cited estimates by the French Minister of Industry that six months' inventory would be sufficient to meet any OPEC threat; Adelman estimated that the per-barrel annual cost of providing six months' storage would be 18 cents.[5] Assuming that the U.S. could purchase the same security by stockpiling a half year's inventory of its imports and that it faced the same 18 cent-per-barrel storage costs, the annual cost of this policy would have been only $170 million in 1967—a cheap price for guaranteeing our oil security.[6] Had the U.S. adopted a stockpiling strategy prior to the 1971 Teheran negotiations, it is doubtful that OPEC would have been bold enough to make its successful blackmail threat. Rather than belabor our past mistake, it is more useful to ask whether stockpiling remains a desirable strategy today.

The oil security of the United States has deteriorated dramatically since 1967. Taken alone, this fact seems to suggest that emergency stockpiling of oil reserves would be an even better strategy today. However, because another consequence of the deterioration of our oil security has been a sharp rise in the stockpiling costs necessary to achieve any specified security increment, the net benefits from adopting a policy of accumulating large stockpiles are, in fact, much more ambiguous today.

There are two reasons why the recent deterioration of U.S. oil security has caused a multifold increase in stockpiling costs. First, it has fostered a sharp rise in the delivered cost of OPEC oil—the only oil available to be stored. Primarily because of this rise, the per-barrel cost of storing oil for six months was at least 30 cents in early 1973.[7] Secondly, a far larger emergency stockpile is now required to provide any specified increment in our oil security— both because interruptions have become much more likely and because our dependence on OPEC oil grows daily. The impact of these two factors is illustrated by the 1973 data. The U.S. will import roughly 2 billion barrels of oil (both crude and products) in 1973. The annual cost of a half year's stockpile of these imports would be about $600 million. Unfortunately, it is no longer clear that a half year's stockpile is adequate: a year's stockpile would cost at least $1.2 billion annually; two years' at least $2.4 billion, etc. Moreover, if the government is roughly correct when it predicts that our relative dependence on foreign oil will rise rapidly over the next few years, the costs of a stockpile necessary to meet an interruption of any specified duration promise to go sharply higher.

Stockpiling of oil has become a relatively high-cost insurance strategy. This fact makes a go-slow approach on stockpiling advisable.[8] Specifically, the government should take immediate steps to undertake preliminary site planning to establish what sites are available for crude oil stockpiling and to initiate low-key negotiations with one or more OPEC members to see if they would sell oil for emergency stockpiles at a discount (or, equivalently, agree to store some of their oil in the U.S. for a few months before delivery to refineries is actually made) in return for a promise to give their oil a far larger share of the U.S. market.[9] (A proposal similar to the second recommendation was apparently made to the U.S., through indirect channels, by a Persian Gulf country in 1969. Thus, the success of some such scheme should not be viewed as totally implausible.) Simultaneously with these negotiations, the U.S. might start to gradually build up its emergency storage capacity.

REDUCING ENERGY DEMANDS

The United States began suffering symptoms of a shortage of refined petroleum products in late 1972; prices of refined products began rising and forced rationing became necessary in numerous markets throughout the country. The shortage of refined products had at least four causes. First, shipments of natural gas, which provide about 32 percent of present U.S. energy needs, showed almost no growth in 1971; they fell slightly in 1972 (chapter 8).

Refined oil products are the only feasible substitute for natural gas over the next few years. Secondly, the enforcement of regional air quality standards and motor vehicle emission standards have both led to higher petroleum demands (chapter 9): the former because several large coal users found that these standards could be satisfied only by switching to low-sulphur residual fuel oil; the latter because they reduced automobile mileage. Third, the economy began growing at an unusually rapid rate in the last quarter of 1972. This growth entailed unusually high energy demands. Finally, and perhaps most importantly, because of the government's oil import controls, refiners were uncertain about where they would be able to secure additional crude oil supplies. As a result of this uncertainty, prudence dictated that they delay making commitments to build new refinery capacity.

Prior to President Nixon's decision to abolish oil import quotas (effective May 1, 1973) no large refinery expansions had been undertaken in the United States for several years. Within six months after oil quotas were abolished, plans for more than 20 large refinery expansions were announced. Unfortunately, because the bulk of these expansion plans cannot be implemented for at least three years, Americans face refined oil products shortages until 1977.

In October 1973, the United States' short-run energy supply position suddenly deteriorated even further when full-scale war erupted between several Arab states (principally Egypt and Syria) and Israel. The fighting was accompanied by an embargo of Arab oil sales aimed at achieving pro-Arab modifications in the major oil consuming nations' foreign policies. As of this writing (late 1973), this embargo prohibits all sales of Arab oil to both the Netherlands and the United States; smaller reductions have been made in sales to other oil-consuming nations.[10]

Rather severe rationing measures are now necessary if the U.S. is to circumvent its immediate oil shortages without undue economic dislocation. The recent ban on Sunday gasoline sales and 15 percent cutback in fuel oil and jet fuel allocations will not be strong enough. Because of the refinery shortage fairly strong rationing measures would have been necessary even if the Arabs had never enforced their embargo.

Unfortunately, public opposition to rationing-caused inefficiencies and inequities will grow as time passes and they become more widely perceived. Thus, additional demand-reducing policies will become both desirable and necessary. Most promising is a high excise tax on all final sales of energy. Such a tax has four justifications:

1. A high energy excise tax will raise energy costs and thereby help to alleviate the present shortage by discouraging consumption.

2. A broad-based energy tax will also reduce consumption of other types of energy besides oil. Because oil is frequently a close substitute for these other energy types, this will help to reduce oil demands. Moreover, since shortages of these other types (especially natural gas) helped to cause our present oil shortage, many will regard a broad-based tax as more equitable than a tax paid exclusively by users of refined oil products.

3. Because U.S. supplies of both low-polluting and secure fuels are severely constrained, environmental pollution and decreased national security are two undesirable by-products of any increase in our energy consumption. Our current and anticipated levels of energy consumption are inefficiently high because the social costs of these two by-products are not reflected in the prices consumers pay. An energy excise tax designed to fully reflect these social costs would help to alleviate these long-run overconsumption problems.

4. An energy excise tax would be cheap to administer. In many cases it could be collected merely by adding a surcharge to existing federal or state taxes.

The most obvious objection to any proposal to levy a large new federal excise tax on energy is that it is not politically feasible. Our politicians are fully aware that most American taxpayers already view themselves as victims of repressive levels of taxation. This objection could be circumvented by granting offsetting reductions in other taxes. Perhaps the best target for reduction would be that component of the Social Security tax paid by employees.[11] This tax was expected to raise about $33 billion during 1973.[12] Because it is a flat-rate tax of 5.85 percent of the first $10,800 of every individual's gross income from earnings (in 1973), and there are no deductions or exemptions, the social security tax has been justly attacked for being highly regressive. Its replacement by a flat-rate tax equal to 33 percent of the gross price (including all existing excise taxes) currently charged on final sales of energy would yield roughly the same total revenue and would almost certainly result in a (slightly) more progressive overall federal tax system.[13] If further progression is desired, tax credits for a minimum necessary level of energy expenditure could be built into the personal income tax.[14]

SUMMARY

The United States is in the midst of a rapidly worsening energy crisis. Its severity is, in large part, the result of past policy omissions and mistakes. Current energy policies have failed to alleviate any of our four energy problems: guaranteeing adequate future supplies of low-cost energy, eliminating the threat of interruptions in the flow of these supplies, reducing energy-related pollution, and preventing the gift of valuable privileges to a select few. In fact, they have actually worsened each of these problems. These policy failures are chiefly due to an inability or unwillingness to coordinate existing policies and a failure to adopt flexible policies responsive to the inevitable changes in the fundamental "facts" upon which they are based. In sum, the crux of the United States' energy crisis lies in the contradiction between economic, political, and technologic realities and our policymakers' inappropriate responses. If the United States is to escape the enervating costs of a perpetual energy crisis, fundamental policy changes must now be made.

NOTES

1. ADEQUATE PROVISION OF LOW-COST ENERGY

1. The relative price of energy began to rise about 1970. Subsequent chapters will explain its causes. This chapter shows that the rise is not due to a growing worldwide physical scarcity.

2. National Science Foundation RANN, *Summary Report of the Cornell Workshop on Energy and the Environment*, p. 153.

3. *Ibid.*, p. 153. It deserves to be emphasized that per capita GNP is now higher in some Western European countries (principally West Germany) than it is in the U.S. Nevertheless, per capita energy consumption is much higher in the U.S. than in these countries.

4. A. P. Lerner, "The Economics and Politics of Consumer Sovereignty," *American Economic Review*, LXII (May, 1972), 258.

5. H. Jackson, "Control of Environmental Hazards," *Michigan Law Review*, LXVIII (1970), 1073–82.

6. United States Council of Economic Advisers, *The Annual Report of the Council of Economic Advisers*, p. 87.

7. D. Meadows et al, *The Limits to Growth*. The basis for this popularized study is J. Forrester, *World Dynamics*. A devastating attack on the nonscientific nature of Forrester-type models has been offered by W. Nordhaus, *World Dynamics: Measurement Without Data*.

8. Meadows, *Limits to Growth*, pp. 132–34, 152.

9. American Petroleum Institute, *Petroleum Facts and Figures*, p. 556.

10. *Ibid.*, p. 544. The increase in reserves was calculated by dividing the sum of total world petroleum reserves in 1969 and total world petroleum consumption between 1944 and 1969 by total world petroleum reserves in 1944.

11. National Petroleum Council, *U.S. Energy Outlook*, II, 155, 172–74.

12. British Petroleum, *BP Statistical Review of the World Oil Industry, 1971*, pp. 4, 8.

13. This example is based upon research reported in J. C. Carr and W. Taplin, *History of the British Steel Industry* and P. Temin, *Iron and Steel in Nineteenth Century America*.

14. Besides being far more efficient than nuclear fission (which is already commercially feasible) the fusion process is preferable because it will not lead to the production of large quantities of dangerous radioactive by-products. Chapter 9 discusses the problem of disposing of radioactive by-products in more detail.

15. Indeed, chapter 2 will explain why, because of the development of the North Sea's recently (since 1970) discovered large oil reserves, Western Europe's dependence on oil imports will fall sharply in the late 1970s.

16. United States Department of Interior, "Detailed Responses to Questions Posed by the Committee on Interior and Insular Affairs."

2. THE SECURITY OF U.S. OIL AND GAS SUPPLIES

1. M. A. Adelman, *The World Petroleum Market*, pp. 45–77.

2. R. B. Mancke, "The Longrun Supply Curve of Crude Oil Produced in the United States," *Antitrust Bulletin*, XV (1970), 727–56.

3. National Petroleum Council, *U.S. Energy Outlook: A Summary Report*, pp. 36, 38. Crude oil's domestic price did rise sharply in late 1973. It will be several years before this leads to higher domestic output.

4. United States Department of Interior, Detailed Responses to Questions Posed by the Committee on Interior and Insular Affairs," p. 4–4. Because of their huge reserves of low cost oil, Iran and (especially) Saudi Arabia are already the most important oil exporters. Their relative importance should grow in the future.

5. United States Cabinet Task Force on Oil Import Controls, *The Oil Import Question*, p. 100.

6. M. A. Adelman, "Is the Oil Shortage Real?" *Foreign Policy*, IX (1972), 76.

7. U.S. Cabinet, *Oil Import Question*, p. 35.   8. *Ibid.*, p. 35.

9. *Ibid.*, pp. 35–36.   10. Adelman, *Petroleum Market*.

11. J. E. Hartshorn, *Politics and World Oil Economics*, pp. 27–28.

12. Canada was (and is) a much higher cost oil producer than the OPEC members.

13. Adelman, *Petroleum Market*, pp. 160–91.

14. Unless they have received direct assistance from federal or state governments, most American cartels have failed. See P. MacAvoy, *Economic Effects of Regulation*.

15. Adelman, "Oil Shortage Real?", pp. 77, 79–84.

16. *Ibid.*, p. 70. Adelman's article prompted a rebuttal by State Department oil advisor James Atkins. Atkins, "The Oil Crisis: This Time the Wolf Is Here," *Foreign Affairs*, LI (April 1973), 462–90.

17. To be effective the OPEC countries would have to cut off sales to all countries. Because such an embargo would be more costly to the more populated OPEC members, they would probably be more reluctant to take this step. Sparsely populated countries like Kuwait and Saudi Arabia are most likely to lead any embargo.

18. "It's Official, Phillips Calls North Sea Oil Field a Giant," *Oil and Gas Journal* (June 8, 1970), p. 81.

19. F. J. Gardner, "Huge North Sea Find has Entire Oil World Vibrating," *Oil and Gas Journal* (May 25, 1970), p. 34.

20. F. J. Gardner, "1972: Year of the Arab," *Oil and Gas Journal* (December 25, 1972), p. 33.

21. "Vast N. Sea Reserves Yet to be Found," *Oil and Gas Journal* (December 4, 1972), p. 33.

22. F. J. Gardner, "Watching the World," *Oil and Gas Journal* (December 4, 1972), p. 47. Industry estimates are at the low end of this range. Barring either a most unlikely political decision to slow down development of the North Sea's crude oil reserves or a sharp fall in the price of foreign oil (presumably because OPEC fails), I suspect that the optimistic estimates are more likely.

3. POLLUTION

1. See K. Arrow, *Social Choice and Individual Values,* for an elegant discussion of this problem.

2. P. Samuelson, "Diagramatic Exposition of a Theory of Public Expenditures," *Review of Economics and Statistics,* XXXVIII (1955), 350–56, offers a more sophisticated discussion.

3. President Eisenhower's Special Health Message (January 31, 1955), H. R. Doc. No. 81, 101 Congressional Record, 997.

4. Act of July 14, 1955, Public Law No. 159, 69 Statute 322. See H. Kennedy and A. Porter, "Air Pollution: Its Control and Abatement," *Vanderbilt Law Review,* VIII (1955), 854–77.

5. Senate Report No. 389, 84th Cong., 1st Sess., p. 3.

6. "Garbage in the Sky," *Fortune,* LI (April, 1955), p. 149.   7. *Ibid.,* p. 174.

8. L. Jaffe, "The Administrative Agency and Environmental Control," *Buffalo Law Review,* XX (1970), 233.

9. H. Jackson, "Symposium: Control of Environmental Hazards," *Michigan Law Review,* LXVIII (1970), 1074.

10. This discussion ignores pollution that is not caused by man or his institutions. For example fire caused by lightning.

11. There is extensive literature on the economics of common property resources. For example see A. Scott, *Natural Resources: The Economics of Conservation,* and S. L. McDonald, *Petroleum Conservation in the United States.*

12. Effluent taxes may not work if the polluter is a public utility allowed to "pass through" to consumers (via rate hikes) higher fuel costs. One way to discourage pollution by utilities is to couple effluent taxes with a proviso allowing all investments for pollution control equipment to be included in the rate base.

13. The mandatory regulations designed to prevent "runaway" offshore oil wells require the use of well-established engineering practices to achieve a rather precise goal.

14. Because of the uncertainty about what is (or will be) the economically most efficient way to control automobile emissions, the mandatory standards legislated for 1975–76 were very unwise. For elaboration see R. B. Mancke, "An Alternative to Auto Emission Control," *California Management Review,* XIV (1972), 82–86. For a slightly different view of possible regulatory options see J. E. Krier and D. Montgomery, "Resource Allocation, Information Cost and the Form of Government Intervention," *Natrual Resources Journal,* XIII.

15. Walter Heller has written a delightful essay on this topic, "Coming to Terms with Growth and the Environment."

16. National Science Foundation RANN, *Summary Report of the Cornell Workshop on Energy and the Environment,* p. IX.

17. It would be possible to list many equally plausible causes of future cataclysms. For example, famine, drought, pestilence, solar eruptions, etc. If we took expensive steps to prevent each one we would die of starvation.

18. Consider the changing importance of an analogous problem: a woman's loss of her virginity prior to marriage. Just a few years ago this was regarded by many elements of our society as very costly. Today the social valuation of virginity does not appear to be nearly so high.

4. DISTRIBUTIONAL CONSEQUENCES OF U.S. OIL AND GAS POLICIES

1. A fascinating account of the events surrounding Andrew Jackson's decision to destroy the Second Bank of the United States may be found in B. Hammond, *Banks and Politics in America,* pp. 326–450.

2. *The Autobiography of Lincoln Steffens.*

3. United States Cabinet Task Force on Oil Import Controls, *The Oil Import Question,* pp. 2–8.

4. "Oil Companies, States Join Import-Quota Battle," *Oil and Gas Journal* (December 25, 1972), p. 45. Together these four states produced 70 percent of all oil produced in the United States during 1969.

5. CONSAD, *The Economic Factors Affecting the Level of Domestic Petroleum Reserves.*

6. CONSAD, "Level of Domestic Petroleum Reserves."

7. "Agreement Helps Clear Way for Alaska Leasing," *Oil and Gas Journal* (September 11, 1972), p. 71.

8. United States Cabinet Task Force on Oil Import Controls, *Estimated Wellhead and Delivered Cost of North Slope Alaskan Crude.* Reprinted in M. A. Adelman, ed., *Alaskan Oil: Costs and Supply,* pp. 71–93.

9. R. B. Mancke, "The Longrun Supply Curve of Crude Oil Produced in the United States," *Antitrust Bulletin,* XV (1970), pp. 727–56.

10. *Ibid.,* p. 747. A forthcoming paper by Thomas Stauffer reportedly estimates even lower domestic oil costs.

11. Specifically, $500 is spent producing 1000 barrels from field A; $1000 is spent producing 1000 barrels from field B, and $1000 is spent producing 500 barrels from field C.

12. Field A's oil costs 50 cents per barrel to produce; therefore, when 1000 barrels are each sold for $2.00, rents are $1500. The total rents earned by fields B and C were calculated in the same fashion.

13. American taxpayers comprise a seventh interest group. However, since this group overlaps with petroleum consumers, I ignore it.

14. If oil producers are competitive and risk neutral, then the winning lease bonus bid would equal the expected present value of the net rents (i.e., the total rents expected to remain after royalties and severance taxes have been paid).

15. The December 1972 federal sale of petroleum rights in the U.S. Gulf netted roughly $1.6 billion. This high return is attributable to the fact that the difference between the revenues expected from the sale of any of this petroleum and its expected costs is high.

16. This discussion is simplified by ignoring the fact that petroleum production is not instantaneous.

17. Persuasive documentation is offered by J. McKie, "Market Structure and Uncertainty in Oil and Gas Exploration," *Quarterly Journal of Economics,* LXXXIV (November 1960), 543–71.

18. For example, those who leased oil land on the Alaskan North Slope prior to the Prudhoe Bay discovery paid only a few pennies per acre. Those who leased the same land after the Prudhoe discovery had to pay several thousand dollars per acre. Those who bought early were "lucky" and will reap high profits if they are allowed to produce this oil.

19. For example, those firms that spent over $900 million buying leases to suspected North Slope oil lands in 1969 (after Prudhoe Bay's discovery) expected that they would be able to start selling this oil in 1973, after the pipeline was built. Delays in the pipeline have resulted in their losing money on these investments.

20. *Oil and Gas Journal* (January 29, 1973), pp. 100–101.

21. Alaska provides the extreme example. No North Slope oil has yet been sold. Nevertheless, the state received lease bonuses of over $900 million in 1969. In 1968 the state government's total expenditures were only $250 million.

22. Consumers have been able to affect natural gas policy. Unfortunately, chapter 8 will show that in this instance their festering hostility toward the "oil interests" has led them to advocate a policy detrimental to their own interests.

5. STATE AND FEDERAL LAND USE POLICIES

1. For more elaboration see A. C. Fisher, J. V. Krutilla, and C. J. Cicchetti, "The Economics of Environmental Preservation," *American Economic Review,* LXII (1972), 605–19.

2. See J. Sax, "Takings, Private Property and Public Rights," *Yale Law Journal,* LXXXI (1971), 149–86.

3. A variety of cost studies are presented in M. A. Adelman, ed., *Alaskan Oil: Costs and Supply.* All estimate that Alaskan oil will cost less than 40 cents per barrel to produce.

4. United States Department of Interior, *An Analysis of the Economic and Security Aspects of the Trans-Alaska Pipeline.*

5. I have been a consultant to a "public interest" law firm representing environmental groups opposed to the trans-Alaskan pipeline. The statement in the text is premised on my

conversations with the concerned lawyers. It deserves to be emphasized that regardless of what route is chosen, costly steps are required to protect the Arctic permafrost.

6. USDI, *Trans-Alaska Pipeline*, I, 6.

7. C. Cicchetti, *Arctic Oil: An Econometric and Environmental Analysis of Alternative Transportation Systems.*

8. USDI, *Trans-Alaska Pipeline*, II, Appendix M–5.

9. *Ibid.*, I, Appendix C, p. 7; and III, Appendix VI.

10. This discussion draws extensively from R. B. Mancke and T. B. Stoel, "Comments on National Security Aspects of Proposed Trans-Alaska Pipeline," and B. Hobbie and R. B. Mancke, "Which Pipeline?" *New Republic*, CLXVI (June 24, 1972), 16–18.

11. The Interior Department (and OEP) failed to note the strongest strictly military argument against the Alaskan pipeline: that a hostile power could disrupt shipments of Alaskan oil for several months (perhaps years) if it were to bomb the key Valdez terminal. Since the Canadian pipeline would not have a single terminus, it would not be vulnerable to such a long-term disruption.

12. *Oil and Gas Journal* (January 15, 1972), p. 62. It deserves to be emphasized that these reserves have not yet been found. Thus, their production lies several years in the future.

13. USDI, *Trans-Alaska Pipeline*, I, Appendix C, p. 14.

14. J. Barnes, ed., *Comments on the Environmental Impact Statement for the Trans-Alaska Pipeline*.

15. The decision to use a common corridor would also lead to sharp reductions in the costs of building and maintaining additional pipelines.

16. A concise discussion of the Teapot Dome scandal may be found in H. Williamson et al., *The American Petroleum Industry*, II, 308–10.

17. The U.S. government uses a lottery to allocate less obvious oil lands. All oil produced is subject to a royalty (16.66 percent of wellhead value) and there is a low annual acreage charge. Rights-of-way for pipelines, etc. are usually granted after payment of a nominal rent.

18. In order to simplify the discussion, all production and sales are assumed to take place instantaneously.

19. When the state uses a combination of fixed royalties and competitive bidding for oil land leases its total rents are measured by the area of trapezoid P_0DCB. These are divided into royalty payments totalling $EDCB$ and lease bonuses totalling P_0DE.

20. Because petroleum comes from heterogeneous land sources and its costs of production change over time, a system of royalties that was not inefficient would have to differ for each land parcel, change over time, and always be zero for each field's marginal barrel.

21. There is a second possible justification not discussed in the text because of its implausibility in the U.S. It is that royalties are used in order to restrict output to the monopoly profit-maximizing level. This justification is unlikely because other policies (especially prorationing and import quotas) have been used to fix prices effectively. See the discussion in chapter 7.

22. A similar proposal has been suggested by J. D. Khazzoom, "The FPC Staff's

Econometric Model of Natural Gas Supply in the United States,'' *Bell Journal of Economics and Management Science,* II (1971), 90–91.

23. This section borrows extensively from M. A. Adelman, "The Efficiency of Resource Use in Crude Petroleum," *Southern Economics Journal,* XXXI (1964), 101–22; W. F. Lovejoy and P. T. Homan, *Economic Aspects of Oil Conservation Regulation;* S. L. Mc-Donald, *Petroleum Conservation in the United States.*

24. Adelman, "Crude Petroleum," p. 101.

25. M. A. Adelman, *The World Petroleum Market,* p. 44.

26. California did not adopt prorationing. The likely explanation for this decision follows: California oil is sold west of the Rockies. Because of high transport costs, the West Coast crude oil market has been (and still is) separate from the market east of the Rockies. Because no large new reserves (i.e., reserves comparable to East Texas) were discovered in California during the 1930s, it did not face similar incentives to adopt prorationing.

27. Implementation of market demand prorationing is slightly more complicated than the text indicates. Two major complications are the result of (1) the exemption of some wells from state prorationing regulations and (2) the fact that not all wells are physically able to produce their allowables.

28. The Connally Hot Oil Act offers an early example of U.S. government aid to the state-run petroleum cartel. This act prohibited the interstate sale of oil above the allowables set by the state prorationing boards.

29. Adelman, "Crude Petroleum," p. 104, estimates that inefficient stripper wells accounted for roughly one-half of all new wells drilled in the early 1960s.

30. Oil import quotas were justified on national security grounds. Beginning in the early 1950s, the states started to use this justification for prorationing. Specifically, they argued that prorationing led to the creation of valuable spare capacity which could be called upon in an emergency. The argument had two flaws: (1) Prorationing is an inefficient way to produce spare capacity and (2) during the oil shortage following the 1956 closing of the Suez Canal, the states did not choose to liberalize prorationing and allow the companies to produce more oil; instead, they allowed oil prices to rise.

31. Adelman estimated (in "Crude Petroleum") that prorationing cost the U.S. about $2.5 billion annually in the early 1960s.

6. TAX INCENTIVES

1. This chapter was coauthored by Christopher Combest.

2. The counterpart of depletion in nonextractive industries is depreciation. The debate over depreciation has generally centered over a choice between straight-line and various alternative methods of calculating accelerated depreciation. The latter may be employed to approximate the rate of deterioration of the asset or simply to give a benefit of deferred tax payment.

3. Cost depletion corresponds directly with capital depreciation—the only difference being that it is variable with the amount of the resource used instead of with time.

4. In the case of oil and gas, "gross revenue" means the value of the oil and gas at the wellhead. Oil and gas, along with sulphur and some rare minerals and metals, receive the

highest allowance. The next highest category of depletable resources receives 15 percent. This category includes oil shale. Coal receives a depletion allowance of 10 percent. See Internal Revenue Code, § 613.

5. B. Bittker and L. Stone, *Federal Income, Estate and Gift Taxation*, p. 332.

6. Internal Revenue Code, §§ 56, 57.

7. *Ibid*, § 263(c). This deduction was authorized by regulations promulgated under the 1918 Act. But, there was no express authorization by Congress until 1945 (House Concurrent Resolution 50, 79:1, *Cum Bull*. 545 [1945]). Congress acted after the Fifth Circuit (in *F.H.E. Oil Company v. Commissioner* 147 F.2nd, 1002, rehearing denied, 149 F.2nd, 238) had held the grant of the option to expense or capitalize contrary to law.

8. Income Tax Regulations, § 612–4(a).   9. *Ibid.*, § 1.613–4(b).

10. Bittker and Stone, *Federal Income*, p. 332.

11. The example discussed in the text simplifies the actual calculation of the percentage depletion deduction by assuming that gross revenues at the wellhead are multiplied by 22 percent. In fact, gross revenues minus royalties is so multiplied. When calculated in this way the deductions remain very close to those shown in the text.

12. This is a well-known engineering rule. It reflects the fact that scale economies are enjoyed when the output of a given well is raised.

13. C. Galvin, "The 'Ought' and 'Is' of Oil-and-Gas Taxation," *Harvard Law Review*, LXXIII (1960), 1441.

14. H.R. Rep. No. 91–413, 91st Cong., 1st Sess., 137 (1969).

15. Sen. Rep. No. 91–552, 91st Cong., 1st Sess., 179 (1969).

16. H.R. Rep. No. 91–782, 91st Cong., 1st Sess., 314 (1969).

17. Bittker and Stone, *Federal Income*, p. 332.

18. The drop in the depletion rate was proportionately less than the drop in the actual amount of the depletion subsidy. This is because at various percentage depletion rates between 27.5 percent and 0 percent, owners of different wells will find it profitable to switch to cost depletion.

19. A short explanation of these complicated tax subsidies is impossible. See Bittker and Stone, *Federal Income*, p. 531.

20. H.R. Rep. No. 91–413, 91st Cong., 1st Sess., 142 (1969).

21. H.R. Rep. No. 91–413, 91st Cong., 1st Sess., 136 (1969).

22. Sen. Rep. No. 91–552, 91st Cong., 1st Sess., 179 (1969).

23. For elaboration of this argument see R. B. Mancke, "The Allocation of U.S. Oil Import Quotas," *Journal of World Trade Law*, VI (1972), 565–73.

24. The depletion allowance is received by petroleum producers. However, since the market for petroleum land rights appears competitive, it appears likely that landowners actually reap the subsidy.

25. CONSAD, "The Economic Factors Affecting the Level of Domestic Petroleum Reserves," p. 83. Based on figures for the mid-1960s: reserves of 31 billion barrels, a price of $2.90 per barrel, and a subsidy cost of $1.2 billion.

7. OIL IMPORT POLICY

1. Principally crude oil producers, oil landowners, and taxpayers residing in the oil states.

2. A variety of factors that initially delayed the influx of oil imports are discussed in M. A. Adelman, *The World Petroleum Market,* pp. 150–56.

3. M. Friedman, "Oil and the Middle East," *Newsweek* (June 26, 1967). Friedman's conclusion was either explicitly or implicitly supported by most of the experts testifying at 1969 hearings before the Senate's Subcommittee on Antitrust and Monopoly.

4. Presidential Proclamation 3279 was issued March 10, 1959. Reprinted in U.S. Cabinet Task Force on Oil Import Controls, *The Oil Import Question,* pp. 197–202.

5. U.S. Cabinet, *Oil Import,* pp. 195–96.

6. The allocation of oil import quota rights was horribly complex; this made their administration cumbersome. Detailed discussion of these complexities may be found in U.S. Cabinet, *Oil Import* and in K. Dam, "Implementation of Import Quotas: The Oil Example," *Journal of Law and Economics,* XIV (April 1971), 1–60.

7. Occidental planned to refine only foreign oil at Machiasport. Thus, if its request were granted, it would still have to purchase 200,000 import rights each day from other refiners.

8. Members of this task force were Secretary of Labor George Shultz (Chairman); Secretary of State William Rogers; Secretary of Treasury David Kennedy, Secretary of Defense Melvin Laird, Secretary of the Interior Walter Hickel, Secretary of Commerce Maurice Stans, Director of Office of Emergency Preparedness George Lincoln. Observers were Director of the Bureau of the Budget Robert Mayo, Chairman of the Federal Power Commission John Nassikas, Assistant Attorney General for Antitrust Richard McClaren, Council of Economic Advisors member Hendrik Houthakker, Special Representative for Trade Negotiations Carl Gilbert, the Office of Science and Technology adviser S. David Freeman. Presidential Assistant Peter Flannigan was the White House liaison.

9. Actually this measure would underestimate the "true" cost of this program because it ignores the "consumers' surplus" which arises because more oil would be consumed at the lower price. The total cost of import quotas could also be calculated by taking the difference between the total cost of crude oil sold in the United States under the mandatory import quota policy and the total cost if this policy had never existed. This would lead to a different cost estimate because the mere existence of import quotas has caused changes in the evolution of the oil industry. For example, if the U.S. had never had oil import quotas, oil transport costs would probably be lower because our ports would have already been expanded to handle supertankers (see chapter 9).

10. U.S. Cabinet, *Oil Import,* pp. 259–63. A similar cost estimate was made by Adelman in 1964. See "Efficiency of Resource Use in Crude Petroleum," pp. 101–22.

11. The United States is subdivided into five Petroleum Administration Districts. See U.S. Cabinet, *Oil Import,* p. 16.

12. This theme is advanced in M. A. Adelman, "Is the Oil Shortage Real?", *Foreign Policy,* IX (1972), 93–94. The fall in the price of residual fuel oil after imports were decontrolled in 1966 supports the argument summarized in the text. Prior to this move, opponents argued that increasing demand due to decontrol would lead to higher residual prices.

13. Actually $P_A Z W P_B$ underestimates the rise in consumer costs attributable to the stricter enforcement of this policy because it ignores the fact that consumers will also be paying more for imported oil. Presently, to take account of this effect, we would need to increase our cost estimates by about 20 percent.

14. The total increase in resource costs would exceed the amount measured by the area of YZW. This amount depends upon the delivered cost of the foreign crude oil that is replaced.

15. U.S. Cabinet, *Oil Import*, pp. 216–25. The recent summary report by the National Petroleum Council implicitly assumes that the long-run elasticity of U.S. crude oil supplies is only 0.34. If correct, the text's estimates of the cost of tighter oil import controls are far too low.

16. U.S. Cabinet, *Oil Import*, p. 261. "The Allocation of U.S. Oil Import Quotas" explains why a large fraction of the value of oil import rights may have been competed away.

17. Besides the reputed power of the "oil lobby," there appear to be two specific political reasons for this rejection: two leading contenders for the 1972 Democratic presidential nomination—Senators Kennedy and Muskie—headed the antiquota opposition and Republican George Bush was thought to have a good chance of winning the Texas Senate seat. In addition, because of delays in construction of the Alaskan pipeline and above-average demand growth, the Oil Import Task Force's projections of U.S. oil import dependence began to look too low almost immediately following release of its study.

18. U.S. Cabinet, *Oil Import*, p. 128.

19. This is because imported oil is most valuable in regions farthest away from the principal sources of domestic oil.

20. A similar argument could be made by residents of the Midwest.

21. Residual fuel oil is used to power and heat utilities, factories, office buildings, apartments, hospitals, schools, etc. It supplies more than 40 percent of the East Coast's needs for such energy. If, for any reason, Venezuela's exports should be interrupted, the U.S. would not have sufficient refinery capacity to process crude oil into residual oil.

22. United States President, *Message from the President of the United States Concerning Energy Resources*, p. 10.

23. *Ibid.*

24. Most important, this policy change effectively eliminates the power of the major oil-producing states to control oil prices by controlling output. Thus, their interest in market demand prorationing should wane.

25. Letter from Senator Henry Jackson to Lewis Engman, Chairman, Federal Trade Commission, in Permanent Subcommittee on Investigations of the Committee on Government Operations United States Senate, Investigation of the Petroleum Industry, (July 12, 1973), p. v.

26. *Preliminary Federal Trade Commission Staff Report on Its Investigation of the Petroleum Industry*, in *Investigation of the Petroleum Industry*, pp. 1–62. It is against FTC policy to release staff studies on matters pending before the FTC. "In the interest of the public's right to know all the facts regarding the fuel shortages," Senator Jackson chose to ignore this policy and release the report.

27. *Ibid.*, p. 43.   28. *Ibid.*, pp. 17, 43.

29. *Investigation of the Petroleum Industry*, p. 15.   30. *Ibid.*, p. 17.

31. When discussing the sliding scale formula the President's Oil Import Task Force wrote: "the smaller refiners are frank to admit that retention of this benefit has been essential to their survival." This hardly supports the FTC's squeezing hypothesis. See U.S. Cabinet, *Oil Import Question*, p. 261.

32. In many instances crude oil producers are not allowed to take the full 22 percent depletion allowance. In such cases royalties and severance taxes will offset more than three-fourths of the tax reduction granted by the depletion allowance.

33. Proof. Let

t = fraction of gross profits retained by a large integrated major after paying all federal profit taxes,

R = the integrated major's total refinery thoughput of crude oil,

C = the integrated major's total crude oil production,

ΔP = change in the price of crude oil,

d = depletion allowance rate,

f = combined rate of state severance taxes and royalties owed the owners of oil lands,

$\Delta \pi_R$ = the change in the integrated major's after-tax profits from refining, and

$\Delta \pi_C$ = the change in the integrated major's after-tax profits from crude oil production.

Suppose the integrated major seeks to shift profits from its refinery operations to its crude operations by raising crude's price. Adoption of this profit-shifting strategy would leave refinery revenues unchanged but refinery costs would rise by (ΔPR) before taxes. Thus, the change in the integrated major's after-tax refining profits will be

$$\Delta \pi_R = - (\Delta PR)t$$

Adoption of this profit-shifting strategy raises pre-tax crude oil revenues by (ΔPC). It also yields a tax reduction because of a rise in the depletion allowance of $d(\Delta PC)$. Partially offsetting the foregoing are higher severance taxes and royalties totaling $f (\Delta PC)$. Thus, the net change in the integrated major's after-tax crude production profits is

$$\Delta \pi_C = (1 - f + d)(\Delta PC)t.$$

Hence, the net profit from adopting this profit-shifting pricing strategy is

$$\Delta \pi_R + \Delta \pi_C = \Delta Pt \; [(1 - f + d)C - R]$$

and, thus, it would be profitable only if

$$[(1 - f + d)C - R] > 0.^{22}$$

If the depletion allowance is 22 percent of the gross wellhead price and the sum of royalties and severance taxes is 15 percent of this price, this inequality will be satisfied only if $\frac{C}{R}$ >0.93. An analagous derivation appears in M. DeChazeau and A. Kahn, *Integration and Competition in the Petroleum Industry* (1959). pp. 221–22. The DeChazeau-Kahn formulation is less general because it ignores severance taxes and royalties. The FTC's study claims, using the DeChazeau-Kahn formulation and thus incorrectly ignoring royalties and severance taxes, that profit-shifting would be profitable as long as an integrated refiner is able to supply more than 40 percent of its crude oil needs. The Commission staff has made a mathematical error. If severance taxes and royalties are ignored and the company is allowed the maximum 22 percent depletion allowance, its crude oil self-sufficiency must exceed 81 percent for profit-shifting to be profitable.

34. The mandatory oil import quotas separated the U.S. market for crude oil from the world market. Thus when seeking to establish under what conditions profit-shifting will be profitable, a firm's production of foreign crude oil should be ignored.

35. A similar argument is offered by C. D. Anderson, "Book Review," *Yale Law Journal,* LXXXII (May, 1973), pp. 1355–62.

36. Assuming that the marginal tax rate on corporate profits is 48 percent, Marathon's after-tax loss because $1 of profits is shifted from refining to crude production is
$$0.52[\$1.07(0.881) - \$1] = -\$0.0298.$$
Standard of Ohio's after-tax loss because $1 of profits are shifted is
$$0.52[\$1.07(0.067) - \$1] = -\$0.483.$$

37. A second conspiracy charge has been offered to explain why several "independent" gasoline dealers (not refiners) were forced to suspend operations in 1973 because they could not obtain adequate supplies. Many asserted that these closings were the result of a "conspiracy" among the major integrated oil companies aimed at eliminating retail competition. The merits of this assertion are dubious. Gasoline was in short supply because of limited refinery capacity. When their product is in short supply, competitive firms find it most profitable to sell to the highest bidder. Failure of a seller to do so would be evidence of a market imperfection. Thus, the fact that "independent" stations were closing because of lack of supplies would offer evidence of a conspiracy if it could be shown that the "majors" denied them oil even though they offered a higher price. But, they could not offer a higher price since the U.S. government had frozen refined product prices below their market clearing level. Given this combination of capacity shortages and frozen prices, even perfectly competitive firms would find it most profitable to allocate their scarce supplies of refined products to their own stations. Hence, the fact that independent dealers were denied supplies offers no evidence of a conspiracy.

8. NATURAL GAS POLICIES

1. This discussion relies heavily on an extensive and excellent collection of secondary sources. One of these, not cited below, is a paper written by Robert Morrow for my University of Michigan Law School seminar: Economics for Public Policy Analysis (Winter 1973).

2. 15 U.S.C.§ 717 Note 3 (1964).   3. *Ibid.*

4. MacAvoy, *Price Formation in Natural Gas Fields,* p. 4.

5. *Phillips Petroleum Co. v. Wisconsin,* 347 U.S. 672 (1954).

6. MacAvoy, *Price Formation,* pp. 252–53.

7. J. B. Dirlam, "Natural Gas: Cost, Conservation, and Pricing," *American Economic Review,* XLVIII (1958), 491.

8. J. D. Khazzoom, "The FPC Staff's Econometric Model of Natural Gas Supply in the United States," *Bell Journal of Economics and Management Science,* II (1971), 55. Khaz-

zoom writes: "We do not have firm evidence on the contribution of each type of drilling (drilling in the search for gas, oil, or petroleum) to non-associated gas discoveries. Preliminary estimates indicate that of the exploratory gas-producing (non-associated) wells that were drilled in 1967, 75 percent were originally drilled in the search for oil. In 1966, this ratio was 40 percent."

9. *Ibid.*, p. 89.

10. Two examples suffice to illustrate the sketchiness of academic evidence about natural gas supplies. (1) Erickson and Spann have provided two of the best studies of natural gas supply. See E. Erickson and R. Spann, "Supply Response in a Regulated Industry: The Case of Natural Gas," *Bell Journal of Economics and Management Science*, II (Spring, 1971), 94–121; R. Spann and E. Erickson, "Joint Costs and Separability in Oil and Gas Exploration," (1973) unpublished. The first concluded that its price-elasticity was 0.69; the second, written just two years later, that it was 3.1. The chief cause of this difference is a specification change. In their first study no constraints were placed on the cross-elasticity of crude oil and natural gas supplies. In the second these cross-elasticities were constrained to be zero. (2) Khazzoom realizes that new field supplies are the strategic variable for natural gas supply. Unfortunately, his econometric model does not deal with discovery but with development because his dependent variable—the American Gas Association's statistics on discoveries in any given year—merely refer to the development of new reserves from new fields. This has little or no relation to what has been discovered that year.

Most past quantitative studies of natural gas supply have limited current relevance for two reasons. First, as Erickson and Spann perceptively point out, because by the late 1960s the U.S. had exhausted its postwar inventory of large gas prospects, new gas supplies have probably become less responsive to price rises. Secondly, most empirical studies of natural gas (and crude oil) supplies are constrained to estimate a constant supply elasticity. To always refer to a single elasticity of gas supply may be misleading because it suggests that this relationship will be unchanged regardless of the level of output and prices. The price-elasticity of natural gas may be very different at the higher prices necessary to equate gas demand and supply. See M. A. Adelman, *The Supply and Price of Natural Gas*, p. 63, n. 2.

11. An excellent analysis of FPC wellhead price regulation may be found in E. Kitch, "Regulation of the Field Market for Natural Gas by the Federal Power Commission," *Journal of Law and Economics*, XI (1968), 243–80.

12. MacAvoy, *Price Formation*, p. 253.   13. Kitch, p. 263.

14. *Atlantic Refining Co. v. Public Service Commission*, 360 U.S. 378 (1959).

15. Other things being equal, gas is more valuable if it is found in large fields or those close to market. Gas from larger fields is more valuable because the producer can guarantee the pipeline larger supplies and this permits it to take advantage of scale economies in gathering facilities.

16. R. S. Spritzer, "Changing Elements in the Natural Gas Picture: Implications for the Federal Regulatory Scheme," *Regulation of the Natural Gas Producing Industy*, ed. Brown, pp. 113–36.

17. See MacAvoy, *Price Formation*, pp. 255–62, for a demonstration. This is the case because restricting output below the market clearing level (i.e., Q_E units) is economically inefficient—the value of each unit up to Q_E exceeds its cost.

18. American Petroleum Institute, *Petroleum Facts and Figures 1971*, p. 24, and Mc-Caslin and West, "U.S. Still Dominates the Free-World Drilling Scene," *Oil and Gas Journal*, (December 4, 1972), p. 23.

19. MacAvoy, *Price Formation.*

20. Because the exploration and development costs of known supplies of both "old" and "associated" gas were incurred sometime in the past, they should now be regarded as fixed. Therefore, the owner of such gas wisely ignores them when deciding how much, if any, of this gas to produce. Instead, he only considers operating costs. Specifically, as long as the additional revenues from producing another barrel of old or associated (i.e., previously developed) gas exceeds the additional operating costs, it is profitable to produce. Quasirents are defined as the excess of revenues over operating costs. The owners of old or associated gas will reap higher quasirents if regulators allow its price to rise. (Note: New investments to explore for and develop an oil or gas field will be made only if the expected present value of that field's quasirents is at least equal to the sum of all expected exploration and development costs. Thus, when considering new petroleum investments, the quasirents necessary to pay back all exploration and development costs ought to be considered part of the supply price.)

21. U.S. President, *Message Concerning Energy Resources,* pp. 3–4.

22. In April 1973 the El Paso Natural Gas Company agreed to import Algerian natural gas. This gas will enter the El Paso system in Texas and will cost $1.57 per Mcf. For details see "New El Paso LNG Project Reveals Soaring Prices," *Oil and Gas Journal* (April 23, 1973), 19.

23. U.S. President, *Message Concerning Energy Resources,* pp. 3–4. The President said:
"I am proposing that gas from new wells, gas newly-dedicated to interstate markets, and the continuing production of natural gas from expired contracts should no longer be subject to price regulation at the wellhead. Enactment of this legislation should stimulate new exploration and development. At the same time, because increased prices on new unregulated gas would be averaged in with the prices for gas that is still regulated, the consumer should be protected against precipitous cost increases.

"To add further consumer protection against unjustified price increases, I propose that the Secretary of the Interior be given authority to impose a ceiling on the price of new natural gas when circumstances warrant. Before exercising this power, the Secretary would consider the cost of alternative domestic fuels, taking into account the superiority of natural gas from an environmental standpoint. He would also consider the importance of encouraging production and more efficient use of natural gas."

9. OTHER POLICIES

1. 46 U.S.C.A. § 861.   2. 46 U.S.C.A. § 883.

3. This is the case even though the U.S. government has granted several subsidies to the merchant fleet. Because of the elimination of competition, these subsidies have been largely retained by the shipping interests.

4. Texas and Louisiana annually ship about 1.3 billion barrels of oil to the U.S. East Coast. Roughly half of this oil is shipped via tanker. More than half would be shipped via tanker if lower cost foreign-flag tankers could be used. The extra cost of shipping a barrel of

oil via U.S.-flag tankers is about 15 cents. Thus, East Coast consumers annually pay about $100 million more for petroleum.

5. The U.S. imported 600 million barrels of non-Canadian crude oil and 847 million barrels of refined products (primarily residual fuel oil) in 1972. Most of the residual and 18 percent of the crude came from the Western Hemisphere. In half of this non-Canadian but Western Hemisphere oil had to be imported on U.S.-flag vessels, the extra cost would have been about $72 million. I.e., $72 million = 0.5[847 million + 0.18 (599 million)] $0.15. If half of the Eastern Hemisphere oil were imported on U.S.-flag vessels, the extra cost would have been about $126 million. I.e., $126 million = 0.5 (389 million) ($0.65). Therefore, $198 million is the higher cost attributable to this "reform." It deserves to be emphasized that these costs would rise sharply over the next few years as oil imports rise and as more of these imports come from more distant Eastern Hemisphere sources. See "U.S. '73 Crude Imports to Jump 31.5%," *Oil and Gas Journal* (April 2, 1973), pp. 34–35.

6. The remainder of this section relies heavily on a paper written by David Young for my seminar on Economics for Public Policy Analysis at the University of Michigan Law School (Winter 1973).

7. It is interesting to note that both oil consumers and producers would suffer from further extensions of the Jones Act. These two groups are not inevitably at loggerheads. See *Oil and Gas Journal* (August 7, 1972), p. 32.

8. Subcommittee on Merchant Marine of the House Committee on Merchant Marine and Fisheries, Hearings on H.R. 10694 and H.R. 10923. 92nd Cong., 1st Sess., 1972.

9. 33 U.S.C.A. §§ 1151–1175.   10. 33 U.S.C.A. § 1161.

11. For a more detailed discussion of the world tanker market see M. A. Adelman, *World Petroleum Market*, pp. 103–30, and the references cited therein.

12. H. S. Marcus, "The U.S. Superport Controversy," *Technology Review,* LXXV (March–April 1973), 49.

13. *President's Energy Message Fact Sheet*, p. 13.

14. The costs of loading and unloading a specified tanker are independent of the length of the trip. There are no large scale economies in these operations.

15. The following discussion relies heavily on a paper written by Tim Whitsitt for my seminar on Economics for Public Policy Analysis at the University of Michigan Law School (Winter 1973). *President's Energy Message Fact Sheet* suggests that the use of supertankers could reduce tanker charges between the Persian Gulf and the U.S. from $1.30 to $0.83 per barrel.

16. To illustrate, Delaware passed a coastal-zone law in 1971 to prohibit heavy industry and offshore bulk transfer terminals from its coastal waters.

17. Marcus, "Superport Controversy," p. 56, and MIT Offshore Oil Task Group, *Georges Bank Petroleum Study,* vol. 2.

18. U.S. Coast Guard, "Deep Water Port Policy Issues," in U.S. Senate Committee on Interior and Insular Affairs, *Deep Water Port Policy Issues,* p. 157.

19. Several factors prompt tankers to flush their tanks during the return voyage to the loading port. First, most tankers carry cargo in only one direction, necessitating a return to the loading port with their tanks in ballast. The seawater that provides the ballast becomes

dirty from mixing with the oil residue that remains clinging to the inside of the tanks even after they have been emptied. This "dirty ballast" has to be disposed of before a new load of crude oil can be picked up. Secondly, some tankers carry a variety of refined products that cannot be mixed. Thus, they are required to arrive at the loading port with clean tanks. Finally, even those tankers which only carry crude oil must wash their tanks periodically because the oily residues, if left to settle in the tanks for too long, become a heavy tarlike sludge. Public awareness of this source of oil pollution of the seas led to the International Convention for the Prevention of Pollution of the Sea by Oil in 1954. This convention established "prohibited zones," generally within 50 miles of any land, for the dumping of oily residues. In 1962 a more efficient method for cleaning and deballasting oil tanks was endorsed by amendments to the Convention. Presently 80 percent of the world's oil transporters have adopted this procedure.

20. MIT, *Georges Bank,* II, 39–40. "Almost all the reported tanker spills are either groundings or collisions in restricted waters, tending to substantiate the low incidence of at-sea, large tanker spills noted in the Coast Guard data."

21. "Plans Advance for Gulf Oil Superports," *Oil and Gas Journal,* pp. 28–29. Onshore storage facilities which are needed to store the oil and transfer it to the Colonial Pipeline for transshipment to the U.S. Midwest would cost an additional $144 million. Similar onshore costs would be required if the artificial island were built.

22. Marcus, "Superport Controversy," p. 57.   23. *Ibid.,* p. 56.

24. Act of December 31, 1970, Public Law No. 91–604, 84 Stat. 1705.

25. U.S. President, *Message Concerning Energy Resources,* p. 7.

26. *Ibid.,* p. 7.

27. J. B. Heywood, "How Clean a Car?" *Technology Review,* LXXIII (July, 1971) 21–29.

28. National Academy of Sciences, *Report by the Committee on Motor Vehicle Emissions,* pp. 5, 102.

29. *Ibid.,* pp. 5, 102.

30. The following discussion benefited from a paper written by Roger Conner for my seminar on Economics for Public Policy Analysis at the University of Michigan Law School (Winter 1973).

31. P. Averitt, "Coal Resources of the United States, January 1, 1967," U.S. Geological Service Bulletin No. 1275 (1969).

32. R. L. Gordon, *"Coal's Role in the Age of Environmental Concern,"* (1973) unpublished, p. 5.

33. In order to obtain this oil savings of 2.5 million barrels per day, all existing boilers capable of using either oil or coal would have to switch to coal and all new fossil fuel boilers would have to be designed to use coal. OEP estimates that an additional 2 million barrels per day of oil could be saved if all dismantling of old, high-cost coal boilers was prohibited and utilities were required to use their coal facilities to provide base load capacity rather than to meet peak load demands. The cost of these changes would be so high that it would be unwise to implement them unless the United States were in the midst of a severe oil shortage. See U.S. Office of Emergency Preparedness, *The Potential for Energy Conservation: Fuel Substitution.*

34. Gordon, "Coal's Role," p. 8.

35. Strip mining for coal on the Western plateau will not be so destructive of the environment. The Western coal lands could be reclaimed at a relatively modest cost. However, since surface rights to Western coal lands can apparently be bought at a fraction of these reclamation costs, opposition to any reclamation is likely to be strong.

36. D. Binder, "A Novel Approach to Reasonable Regulation of Strip Mining," *University of Pittsburgh Law Review,* XXXIV (1973), 348.

37. MIT, *Georges Bank* is the most comprehensive study of the environmental effects of offshore drilling. This study concluded (Summary, p. 83): "We were unable to identify any environmental effect associated with offshore oil production which appears likely to materially upset the Georges Bank ecosystem."

38. The following discussion relies heavily on papers written by William Edmunds and Michael Nelson. Edmund's paper was written for my Industrial Organization course (1973); Nelson's was written for my Economics for Public Analysis (Winter 1973).

39. The technological breakthrough for a controlled nuclear fusion reaction has yet to take place. Thus, fusion does not promise to be a commercial source of power for at least 20 to 30 years. If fusion is technologically and commercially feasible, it will not be plagued by most of the waste disposal problems plaguing fission reactors.

40. A. Hammond, "Fission: The Pro's and Con's of Nuclear Power," *Science,* CLXXVIII (October 13, 1972), 147–149.

41. A. Weinberg, "Social Institutions and Nuclear Energy," *Science,* CLXXII (July 7, 1972), 28.

42. These tanks have already sprung at least nine leaks.

43. C. Starr and R. P. Hammond, "Nuclear Waste Storage," *Science,* CLXXVII (September 1, 1972), 744.

44. Plutonium was shipped by air until a plane containing some was hijacked to Cuba.

45. Briefly, the reasons for the difference are as follows: The light water reactor is inherently stable. If the system overheats and the water coolant boils away, there is less moderation so neutron velocity is increased. Since the fuel used (uranium 235) is more likely to intercept slow neutrons, increased neutron velocity results in fewer emissions and the reaction is slowed. On the other hand, the fast breeder reactor will use fast neutrons, so if neutron velocity is increased through a loss of coolant, the reaction speeds up.

46. R. Gillette, "Nuclear Safety III: Critics Charge Conflict of Interest," *Science,* CLXXVII (September 15, 1972), 974.

47. President Nixon issued his second energy message of 1973 on June 29. He asked Congress for a five-year, $10 billion energy research program to be run by a new Energy Research and Development Administration (ERDA). Because most of this money is expected to be used to press development of coal liquidification or gasification and the fast breeder reactor, I think it unwise. The criticism by Edward E. David, President Nixon's former Science Adviser, also bears repetition: "High technology will not play the central role in assuring our energy supply that it did in the space and military programs of the 1960's. A different strategy is called for—one in which federally-funded research and development will play a lesser role and in which the single-minded federal agency is not a

feasible approach." See E. E. David, "Energy: A Strategy of Diversity," *Technology Review,* LXXV (June 1973), 26.

10. REFORMING EXISTING ENERGY POLICIES

1. United States President, *Executive Order Establishing a Special Committee on Energy and National Energy Office.*

2. Evidence that coordination will prove difficult came late in June 1973, when the President announced that he was abolishing his three-month-old Special Committee on Energy and replacing it with an Energy Policy Office under the direction of one man (initially Colorado Governor John Love). The President also announced that he would seek congressional approval for a new Department of Energy and Natural Resources which would assume responsibility for administering most energy policies. A similar proposal was sent to Congress in 1971. No action was taken.

3. United States President, *Message Concerning Energy Resources,* p. 4.

4. R. B. Manke, "The Longrun Supply Curve of Crude Oil Produced in the United States," *Antitrust Bulletin,* xv (1970), 745–48.

5. From 1957 through 1971 there were only two spills from offshore towers of over one million gallons. Unfortunately, both occurred in the U.S. in 1970. Over the same period there were only 23 spills from all sources, including tankers, in excess of one million gallons. These figures are for the entire world, not just the U.S. See MIT Offshore Oil Task Group, *Georges Bank Petroleum Study,* II, 14–17.

6. This conclusion accords with the conclusions found in MIT, *Georges Bank.* Technically the Santa Barbara spill was not caused by a "blowout." Instead, the cause was faulty well casing. Specifically, an upper strata which was open to the ocean floor at points some distance from the well became pressurized because faulty well casing allowed communication between it and a high-pressure lower strata.

11. NEW POLICIES

1. In fact, implementation of the counter-cartel would seem to require granting the multinational oil companies at least a partial immunity from U.S. antitrust laws. Thus, it is possible that these companies would be the chief beneficiaries of the counter-cartel. That is, it could be used to advance their interests rather than the interests of the consuming countries.

2. M. A. Adelman, "Is the Oil Shortage Real?", *Foreign Policy,* IX (1972), 87–88.

3. In a statement recently submitted to the Senate, Professor Adelman also expresses some doubt about the efficacy of his suggestion: "It will be more difficult to get the cartel out of the driver's seat than it was for our government to put it in power. It would not help to get American corporations out of their key . . . [rent] collecting role by a unilateral act. Other nations would replace them." United States Senate Committee on Interior and Insular Affairs, *Oil and Gas Import Issues,* III, 1052–53.

4. Some have suggested that the federal government should enter the business of producing oil and gas for sale. This would provide additional "insurance" only if the federal government produced oil that would not be produced by private companies. Such oil would be very high cost. Thus, I would oppose this policy unless convincing evidence is presented that public production of energy is preferable to private production.

5. M. A Adelman, *World Petroleum Market*, 265–75, estimates that annual storage costs were about 35 cents per barrel. This estimate was arrived at by adding 5-cent annual operating costs to annualized capital costs of 30 cents. The annualized capital costs were premised on the assumptions that 10 percent was the appropriate discount rate, facilities capable of storing oil for 25 years cost $1.25 per barrel to construct, and the delivered cost of the oil to be stored was $1.65 per barrel.

6. U.S. imports of crude and products totalled 925,911,000 barrels in 1967. If it cost 18 cents to store a barrel for a half a year, total storage costs would have been $166,663,980.

7. I estimate that annual storage costs were about 60 cents per barrel in Spring 1973. This estimate was arrived at by adding annual operating costs of 5 cents to annual capital costs of 58 cents. My estimate of annual capital costs is higher than Adelman's 1967 estimate because I assumed the delivered cost of OPEC oil has risen from $1.65 to $3.50 per barrel and the discount rate has risen from 10 to 12 percent.

8. As a practical matter, implementation of any large-scale stockpiling strategy is likely to be delayed by a lengthy round of environmental litigation aimed at challenging huge stockpiles as an appropriate land use.

9. If some OPEC members would agree to delay collecting royalties on any oil stored in the U.S. until it was used, annual per-barrel storage costs could be reduced by about 20 cents.

10. A selective Arab embargo aimed only at reducing the oil supplies of the U.S. cannot work. Already some non-Arab oil that would have otherwise been consigned to Western European or Japanese ports has simply been diverted to the U.S. Thus, any shortfall of world oil supplies will be borne by all of the large oil consumers.

11. Other possibilities include allowing additional large credits on the federal income tax and rebating a large fraction of energy tax revenues to state and local governments so that they can, in turn, cut property taxes.

12. The 1973 *Annual Report of the Council of Economic Advisers* estimates that 1973 Social Security receipts will total $64.5 billion. Roughly half of these will be paid by employees.

13. The retail value of all energy consumed in the United States (including all excise taxes) during 1973 should be about $100 billion. Thus, a 33 percent surcharge should raise about $33 billion.

14. If it is felt that the proposed high energy surcharge would hurt some people, credits should also be allowed on the personal income tax. For example, the first $100 of a family's annual heating bill might be allowed as a tax credit.

BIBLIOGRAPHY

Adelman, Morris A., ed. *Alaskan Oil: Costs and Supply.* New York: Praeger, 1971.
——. "Efficiency of Resource Use in Crude Petroleum," *Southern Economics Journal,* XXXI (1964).
——. "Is the Oil Shortage Real?" *Foreign Policy,* IX (1972).
——. "Statement," in United States Senate Committee on Interior and Insular Affairs. *Oil and Gas Imports Issues.* Part 3. Washington, 1973.
——. *The Supply and Price of Natural Gas.* Oxford: Basil Blackwell, 1962.
——. *The World Petroleum Market.* Baltimore: Johns Hopkins Press, 1972.
American Petroleum Institute. *Petroleum Facts and Figures.* Washington: American Petroleum Institute, 1971.
Anderson, C. David. "Book Review," *Yale Law Journal,* LXXXII (May, 1973).
Arrow, Kenneth. *Social Choice and Individual Values.* New York: Wiley, 1951.
Atkins, James. "The Oil Crisis: This Time the Wolf Is Here," *Foreign Affairs,* LI (April, 1973).
Averitt, Paul. "Coal Resources of the United States, January 1, 1967," in U.S. Geological Service Bulletin No. 1275, (1969).
Barnes, James, ed. *Comments on the Environmental Impact Statement for the Trans-Alaska Pipeline.* Washington: Wilderness Society, 1972.
Binder, Denis. "A Novel Approach to Reasonable Regulation of Strip Mining." *University of Pittsburgh Law Review,* XXXIV (1973).
Bittker, Boris, and Lawrence Stone. *Federal Income, Estate and Gift Taxation.* Boston: Little Brown, 1972.
British Petroleum. *BP Statistical Review of the World Oil Industry, 1971.* London: Brittanic House, 1972.
Carr, J. C., and W. Taplin. *History of the British Steel Industry.* Oxford: Basil Blackwell, 1962.
Cicchetti, Charles. *Arctic Oil: An Econometric and Environmental Analysis of Alternative Transportation Systems.* Washington: Resources for the Future, 1973.
CONSAD Research Corporation, "The Economic Factors Affecting the Level of Domestic Petroleum Reserves." In U.S. Congress Committee on Ways and Means and Senate Committee on Finance. *Tax Reform Studies and Proposals.* Part 4. Washington, 1969.

Dam, Kenneth. "Implementation of Import Quotas: The Oil Example." *Journal of Law and Economics*, XIV, (1971).

David, Edward E. "Energy: A Strategy of Diversity." *Technology Review*, LXXV (June 1973).

DeChazeau, Melvin and Alfred Kahn. *Integration and Competition in the Petroleum Industry*. New Haven: Yale University Press, 1959.

Dirlam, Joel B. "Natural Gas: Cost, Conservation, and Pricing." *American Economic Review*, XLVIII (1958).

Erickson, Edward, and Robert Spann. "Supply Response in a Regulated Industry: The Case of Natural Gas." *Bell Journal of Economics and Management Science*, II (1971).

Fisher, A. C., J. V. Krutilla, and C. J. Cicchetti. "The Economics of Environmental Preservation." *American Economic Review*, LXII (1972).

Forrester, Jay. *World Dynamics*. Cambridge: Wright Allen, 1971.

Friedman, Milton. "Oil and the Middle East." *Newsweek* (June 26, 1967).

Galvin, Charles. "The 'Ought' and 'Is' of Oil-and-Gas Taxation." *Harvard Law Review*, LXXIII (1960).

Gillette, Robert. "Nuclear Safety III: Critics Charge Conflict of Interest." *Science*, CLXXVII (September 15, 1972).

Hammond, Allen. "Fission: The Pro's and Con's of Nuclear Power." *Science*, CLXXVIII (October 13, 1972).

Hammond, Bray. *Banks and Politics in America*. Princeton: Princeton University Press, 1957.

Hartshorn, J. E. *Politics and World Oil Economics*. New York: Praeger, 1967.

Heller, Walter. "Coming to Terms with Growth and the Environment." In Sam Schurr, ed., *Energy, Economic Growth and the Environment*. Baltimore: Johns Hopkins Press, 1972.

Heywood, John B. "How Clean a Car?" *Technology Review*, LXXIII (July, 1971).

Hobbie, Barbara, and Richard B. Mancke. "Which Pipeline?" *The New Republic*, CLXVI (June 24, 1972).

Jackson, Henry. "Control of Environmental Hazards," *Michigan Law Review*, LXVIII (1970).

Jaffe, Louis. "The Administrative Agency and Environmental Control." *Buffalo Law Review*, XX (1970).

Kennedy, Harold, and Andrew Porter, "Air Pollution: Its Control and Abatement." *Vanderbilt Law Review*, VIII (1955).

Khazzoom, J. Daniel. "The FPC Staff's Econometric Model of Natural Gas Supply in the United States." *Bell Journal of Economics and Management Science*, II (1971).

Kitch, Edmund. "Regulation of the Field Market for Natural Gas by the Federal Power Commission." *Journal of Law and Economics*, XI (1968).

Krier, James E., and David Montgomery. "Resource Allocation, Information Cost and the Form of Government." *Natural Resources Journal*, XIII (January, 1973).

Lerner, Abba P. "The Economics and Politics of Consumer Sovereignty." *American Economic Review*, LXII (1972).

Lovejoy, W. F., and P. T. Homan. *Economic Aspects of Oil Conservation Regulation*. Baltimore: Johns Hopkins University Press, 1967.

MacAvoy, Paul. *Economic Effects of Regulation*. Cambridge: MIT Press, 1965.

——. *Price Formation in Natural Gas Fields*. New Haven: Yale University Press, 1962.

McDonald, Stephen L. *Petroleum Conservation in the United States*. Baltimore: Johns Hopkins University Press, 1971.

McKie, James. "Market Structure and Uncertainty in Oil and Gas Exploration." *Quarterly Journal of Economics*, LXXXIV (1960).

Mancke, Richard B. "The Allocation of US Oil Import Quotas." *Journal of World Trade Law*, VI (1972).

———. "An Alternative to Auto Emission Control." *California Management Review*, XIV (1972).

———. "The Longrun Supply Curve of Crude Oil Produced in the United States." *Antitrust Bulletin*, XV (1970).

———., and Thomas B. Stoel. "Comments on National Security Aspects of Proposed Trans-Alaska Pipeline." In James Barnes, ed., *Comments on the Environmental Impact Statement for the Trans-Alaska Pipeline*. Washington: Wilderness Society, 1972.

Marcus, Henry S. "The U.S. Superport Controversy." *Technology Review*, LXXV (March–April, 1973).

Massachusetts Institute of Technology Offshore Oil Task Group. *The Georges Bank Petroleum Study*. 3 vols. Cambridge: MIT Press, 1973.

Meadows, Donella et al. *The Limits to Growth*. New York: New American Library, 1972.

Morton, Roger G. "Statement," in U.S. Senate Committee on Interior and Insular Affairs, *Hearings*. Washington, June 15, 1971.

National Academy of Sciences. *Report by the Committee on Motor Vehicle Emissions*. Washington, 1973.

National Petroleum Council. *U.S. Energy Outlook*. Washington: National Petroleum Council, 1971.

National Petroleum Council. *U.S. Energy Outlook: A Summary Report*. Washington: National Petroleum Council, 1972.

National Science Foundation RANN. *Summary Report of the Cornell Workshop on Energy and the Environment*. Washington: Government Printing Office, 1972.

Nordhaus, William. *World Dynamics: Measurement Without Data*. New Haven: Cowless Foundation, 1973.

Samuelson, Paul. "Diagrammatic Exposition of a Theory of Public Expenditures." *Review of Economics and Statistics*, XXXVII (1955).

Sax, Joseph. "Takings, Private Property and Public Rights." *Yale Law Journal*, LXXXI (1971).

Scott, Anthony. *Natural Resources: The Economics of Conservation*. Toronto: University of Toronto Press, 1955.

Spritzer, Ralph S. "Changing Elements in the Natural Gas Picture: Implications for the Federal Regulatory Scheme." In Keith C. Brown, ed., *Regulation of the Natural Gas Producing Industry*. Baltimore: Johns Hopkins Press, 1971.

Starr, Chauncey, and R. Phillip Hammond. "Nuclear Waste Storage." *Science*, CLXXVII (September 1, 1972).

Steffens, Lincoln. *The Autobiography of Lincoln Steffens*. New York: Harcourt, 1931.

Temin, Peter. *Iron and Steel in Nineteenth Century America*. Cambridge: MIT Press, 1964.

United States Cabinet Task Force on Oil Import Controls, *Estimated Wellhead and Delivered Cost of North Slope Alaskan Crude*. Washington, 1969.

United States Cabinet Task Force on Oil Import Controls. *The Oil Import Question*. Washington: Government Printing Office, 1970.

United States Council of Economic Advisers. *The Annual Report of the Council of Economic Advisers.* Washington: Government Printing Office, 1971.

United States Department of Interior. *An Analysis of the Economic and Security Aspects of the Trans-Alaska Pipeline.* Washington, 1972.

United States Department of Interior. "Detailed Responses to Questions Posed by the Committee on Interior and Insular Affairs." In U.S. Senate Committee on Interior and Insular Affairs. *Hearings.* Washington, January 1973.

United States Office of Emergency Preparedness. *The Potential for Energy Conservation: Fuel Substitution.* Washington: Government Printing Office, 1972.

United States President. *Executive Order Establishing a Special Committee on Energy and National Energy Office.* Washington, April 18, 1973.

——. *Message from the President of the United States Concerning Energy Resources.* Washington, April 18, 1973.

United States Senate Committee on Interior and Insular Affairs. *Deep Water Port Policy Issues.* Washington: Government Printing Office, 1972.

United States Senate Subcommittee on Antitrust and Monopoly. *The Petroleum Industry: Economists' Views.* Washington, 1969.

United States Senate Subcommittee on Investigations of the Committee on Government Operations. *Investigation of the Petroleum Industry.* Washington, July 12, 1973.

Weinberg, Alvin. "Social Institutions and Nuclear Energy." *Science,* CLXXII (July 7, 1972).

Williamson, Harold, Ralph Andreano, Arnold Daum, and Gilbert Klase. *The American Petroleum Industry.* 2 vols. Evanston, Ill.: Northwestern University Press, 1963.

INDEX TO
THE FAILURE OF
U.S. ENERGY POLICY

Adelman, Morris A., 27, 28, 156

Alaskan North Slope, 36, 37, 48, 49, 60 ff.

Alaskan pipeline, 36, 53, 60 ff.; cost of, 62 ff.

Alternative types of energy, 4, 13; long-run, 5, 6; short-run, 5

Antitrust, 100 ff.

Arab states, wars involving, 21, 26, 32, 124, 142, 160

Atomic Energy Commission, 134, 138, 151

Balance of payments, 33

Charcoal, 11 ff.

Clean Air Act of 1970, 39, 129

Coal, 12, 14, 118, 131 ff.; conversion to gas, 131

Coke, 12, 13

Competition, description of, 26

Congress, U.S., 37, 118, 119, 123

Conspiracy, 100 ff.

Costs: of producing crude oil, 18, 48 ff., 118; resource, 48 ff.; of producing natural gas, 109 ff., 116, 118, 119

Council of Economic Advisers, U.S., 7

Counter-cartel, 155, 156

Crude oil, 3 ff., 142; consumption, 10, 11, 14, 18; production, 10, 11, 18, 48 ff.; sources, 10, 14, 18 ff., 60 ff., 88 ff.; reserves, 10, 11, 14, 24, 25, 148; imports, 14 ff., 17 ff., 20, 33, 34, 75, 88 ff.; productivity of wells, 18 ff., 48 ff.; costs, 18 ff., 48 ff., 118; embargoes of, 30, 31, 34, 89, 160; North Sea production, 31, 32; offshore, 148, 149

East Texas, 73, 88

Emission standards, 39, 129 ff., 150

Energy conservation, 5, 6; desirability of, 43; crisis, 73, 74

Energy consumption, intercountry differences, 4, 5; shortages, 13 ff., 18, 21 ff., 62 ff., 99 ff., 104 ff., 115, 116, 159 ff.

Energy demand, growth in U.S., 3; relationship to GNP growth, 3, 5; relationship to price, 4 ff., 11; reductions in, 159 ff.

Energy supply, 141 ff.; different types of energy, 3, 4; quantities, 9, 11; underestimates of, 9, 10; short-term, 13 ff.

Environmental Protection Agency, 39, 129 ff.

Environmental restraints, 36 ff.; delays due to, 14, 61 ff.; enforcement costs, 39, 42

Federal Power Commission, 107, 118, 147

Friedman, Milton, 89

Galvin, Charles, 83

GNP growth, 3

Growth, desirability of, 6 ff.; criticisms of, 7; limits to, 8 ff.; causes of, 9

Income distribution, 46 ff.; transfer payments, 47, 48, 68, 93 ff., 109, 113 ff., 143

Interest groups, 51 ff., 92 ff.; landowners, 52, 72 ff.; producers, 52, 53, 72 ff.; oil-producing states, 53, 54, 72 ff.; refiners, 54; suppliers of services, 54; consumers, 54, 55

International oil companies, 27

Interstate Oil Compact Commission, 75

Israel, wars involving, 21, 26, 32, 33, 124, 142, 160

Jackson, Senator Henry, 7

Jaffe, L., 38

Jones Act, 122 ff., 147; enforcement costs, 123 ff.

Land use, 59 ff.; public lands definition of, 59, 60

Lease bonuses, 52, 61, 68 ff., 148

Lerner, Abba P., 6, 7

MacAvoy, Paul, 108, 117

Malthusian arguments, 8 ff.; evaluation of, 44

Monopoly, OPEC, 26 ff.; OPEC profits, 30; domestic conspiracy, 100 ff.

Nationalization, 42

National security, U.S., 32, 33, 142, 154 ff.; threats posed by oil import interruptions, 16, 21 ff., 30, 31, 34, 89, 160; dependence on Soviet oil, 33, 34; dependence on Soviet natural gas, 119; Jones Act, 122 ff.

Natural gas, 3 ff., 47, 48, 61, 106 ff., 142; transmission, 106 ff.; sources, 106, 118; demand, 106, 107; regulation of, 107 ff., 117, 147; price regulation, 107 ff.; responsiveness to price, 109 ff.; costs, 109 ff., 116, 118, 119; long-run supply, 115; supplemental sources, 118, 119; policy options, 118 ff.

Natural Gas Act of 1938, 107 ff.

North Sea, 31, 32

Nuclear energy, 134 ff.; fusion, 11; fission, 14, 134; Atomic Energy Commission, 134, 138, 151; light water reactor, 134 ff., 151; safety of, 135 ff., 151; theft of, 136 ff., 151

Oil depletion allowance, 17, 47, 77 ff., 101 ff., 146

Oil import controls, 89 ff., 149; quotas, 17, 89 ff., 101 ff., 149, 160; opposition to, 47; cost of, 89 ff., tariffs, 149

Oil imports, 14 ff., 17 ff., 75, 88 ff.;

interruptions of, 15, 16, 21 ff., 30, 31, 142; projections of, 19, 22, 23; from U.S.S.R., 33, 34

Oil Import Task Force, U.S., 49, 90 ff.

Oil shale, 10, 11

Organization of Petroleum Exporting Countries, 19, 21, 149, 150, 154 ff.; oil monopoly, 26 ff.; formation of, 27, 28; goals of, 27 ff.; members of, 27, 28; success of, 28 ff.; dangers posed by, 28 ff., 34, 154 ff.; effect on balance of payments, 33; counter-cartel, 155, 156

Outer continental shelf, 148, 149

Persian Gulf, oil imports from, 17 ff., 88, 89; oil reserves, 18, 19

Pig iron, 11 ff.

Policymakers, 143 ff.; responsibilities, 6, 8, 35, 46 ff.; problems facing, 36 ff., 43 ff., 51 ff., 142; President, 37, 89 ff., 96 ff., 118, 126, 130, 144, 149, 160; Congress, 37, 118, 119, 123; Federal Power Commission, 107 ff., 118, 147; Environmental Protection Agency, 39, 129 ff.; Atomic Energy Commission, 134, 138, 151

Pollutants, definition of, 35; air, 37 ff., 129 ff., 150; automobile, 38, 130, 131; radiation, 40, 135 ff., sulphur oxides, 40 ff., 129, 135; oil spills, 59, 64 ff., 127; coal, 131 ff.; thermal, 134

Pollution, 35 ff.; social costs, 35 ff., 38, 135; causes, 39 ff.; policies to alleviate, 40 ff., 142, 150

President, U.S., 37, 89 ff., 96 ff., 118, 126, 130, 144, 149, 160

Prices, energy, 3 ff., 9 ff.; world oil, 18 ff., 28; oil, 73 ff., 88 ff.; natural gas, 107 ff., 112 ff.

Privileges, 46 ff., 143; definition of, 46; recipients of, 51 ff.

Profits, OPEC, 30; domestic, 89 ff.

Prorationing, 72 ff., 88, 145, 146

Prudhoe Bay, 36, 37, 60 ff.

Public lands, 59 ff.

Rationing, 160 ff.

Refineries, expanding capacity, 160

Regulation, 42

Rents, 18 ff., 61, 88, 148; collection of, 60, 68; natural gas, 109

Residual fuel oil, 98

Resource exhaustion, 8 ff., 13

Royalties, 27, 68 ff.; lease bonuses, 52, 53, 68 ff.; severance taxes, 53, 54, 68 ff.

Santa Barbara, 59

Stockpiling oil, 157 ff.

Strip mining, 133

Subsidies, 41, 42, 77 ff.

Superports, 125 ff., 150; port congestion, 127, 128

Supertankers, 125 ff.

Tarsands, 10, 11

Taxes, 41, 42, 77 ff., 146, 147; severance taxes, 53, 54; percentage depletion, 77 ff., 146; Reforms Act of 1969, 78, 84 ff.; quick expensing, 79, 146; energy excise tax, 161 ff.

Technological constraint, crude oil, 48, 49; natural gas, 48, 49

Technological uncertainty, 11, 43 ff.

Unitization laws, 41; need for, 72 ff.

Wars, 142; involving U.S., 21; regional wars, 21, 26; between Arabs and Israel, 21, 26, 32, 33, 124, 160